Advance Praise for *Ready, Set, Go Lead!*

"*Ready, Set, Go Lead!* is contemporary, accessible   and
grounded in scholarship. It's a really u~~ ~   \ders."

CN
De   'th
Head, WHO Collaborating Centre for .   , ...ent
                                            ...iology, Sydney
                                            Kuring-Gai Campus
                                            Australia

"*Ready, Set, Go Lead!* captures the basics needed to launch or strengthen a
career that will require leadership. The common sense strategies that are
provided are evidence-based and readily applicable to any practice setting.
This book should be included in the required reading list for anyone who wishes
to develop the skills required to be a leader."

—Linda Q. Everett, PhD, RN, FAAN
Executive Vice President, Chief Nurse Executive
Clarian Health Partners
Indianapolis, Indiana, USA

"Consistent with her deep commitment to, and passion for, influential nursing
leadership, Nancy Dickenson Hazard's latest contribution to the literature, *Ready,
Set, Go Lead!* is a welcome source of knowledge and inspiration. In this concise
and easy-to-read handbook, Hazard shares key leadership lessons through
illustrative and exhilarating stories reflective of her professional nursing career
as teacher, mentor, and executive. In an age when emerging nurse leaders are the
key to the future, *Ready, Set, Go Lead!* offers the finest instruction for novice
and expert alike on the art and skill of nursing leadership."

—Jeanette Ives Erickson, RN, MS, FAAN
Senior Vice President for Patient Care Services
Chief Nurse Executive
Massachusetts General Hospital
Boston, Massachusetts, USA

"Reading the first chapters of this book made me want to read more. It clearly
shows the broad spectrum of activities required by leaders in complex
disciplines such as nursing. The main messages are clear and straightforward
yet set against relevant background information that interested readers can
follow up as required."

—Valerie Fleming, RN, RM, MA, PhD
Director, WHO Collaborating Centre
Professor and Head of Division
School of Nursing, Midwifery and Community Health
Glasgow Caledonian University
Glasgow, Scotland

Ready, Set, Go Lead!

Nancy Dickenson-Hazard, RN, MSN, FAAN

Sigma Theta Tau International
Honor Society of Nursing®

Sigma Theta Tau International

Editor-in-Chief: Jeff Burnham
Acquisitions Editor: Cynthia Saver, RN, MS
Project Editor: Carla Hall
Copy Editor: James E. Mattson
Proofreaders: Paula Jeffers, Jane Palmer

Cover Design: Gary Adair
Interior Design and Page Composition: Gary Adair
Printed in the United States of America
Printing and Binding: Printing Partners

Sigma Theta Tau International
550 West North Street
Indianapolis, IN 46202

Visit our Web site at www.nursingknowledge.org/STTI/books for more information on our books.

ISBN-13: 978-1-930538-74-0
ISBN-10: 1-930538-74-X

Library of Congress Cataloging-in-Publication Data

Dickenson-Hazard, Nancy.
  Ready, set, go lead! : a primer for emerging health care leaders / Nancy Dickenson-Hazard.
      p. cm.
  Includes bibliographical references and index.
  ISBN-13: 978-1-930538-74-0 (1-930538-74-x)
  ISBN-10: 1-930538-74-X
  1. Leadership. 2. Health services administration. I. Title.
  HD57.7D54 2008
  362.1068'4--dc22
                          2008036755

08   09   10   11   12   /   5   4   3   2   1

Dedication

For John, Anne, John B, Katy, and Marcia for always being the wind beneath my wings. And, of course, for Carmen and Blaine who started it all.

About the Author

Nancy A. Dickenson-Hazard, RN, MSN, FAAN

Nancy Dickenson-Hazard is the principal of NDH Agency, a consulting firm that specializes in leadership, innovation, and executive coaching. Her services have been used by the World Health Organization, Sigma Theta Tau International, and the Oncology Nursing Society.

From her early career caring for the impoverished children of Appalachia to her current role, Dickenson-Hazard has been a leader—creating and driving initiatives that directly impact patient care and professional issues. One of her strongest skills is collaborative leadership. She is a synthesizer—listening, summarizing, and finding common ground that is not always obvious. She has written extensively on leadership and is an adjunct faculty at the Indiana University School of Nursing and the University of Western Sydney School of Nursing in Australia.

Dickenson-Hazard served as chief executive officer of the Honor Society of Nursing, Sigma Theta Tau International, for 14 years. Under her leadership, the honor society almost tripled its asset base and experienced a 40 percent growth in membership and 26 percent increase in established chapters. She initiated an international nursing leadership institute, established an international think-tank conference series, developed partnerships with the World Health Organization, Monster Jobs, People to People, Johnson and Johnson, and the International Council of Nurses, and developed technologically driven information and knowledge resources used by nurses globally. Her extensive track record in leadership includes a dozen years as executive director of the National Certification Board of Pediatric Nurse Practitioners and Nurses, where she played an instrumental role in securing increased funding for advanced practice nurse education, prescriptive authority, and reimbursement at the national level.

Dickenson-Hazard received her bachelor's degree in nursing from the University of Kentucky and her master's in nursing from the University of Virginia College of Nursing.

About the Cover

The crane symbolizes honor and loyalty, two outcomes people on their leadership journeys hope to achieve.

Table of Contents

Foreword

"[This book] is not so much a focus on leadership skills alone but instead centers more on the person of the leader and the expression of the role as a manifestation of who the leader is rather than simply what the leader does."

I am fortunate to have worked with Nancy Dickenson-Hazard in a number of different roles and forums over the past two decades and have both benefited and learned from her special leadership attributes. This wonderful compilation of straightforward leadership elements and characteristics helps the reader glimpse into the spirit and application of solid leader skills. Written in a personal style, this book reflects the warmth and approach of the author. Anecdotes provide exemplars of application and serve as a window into the value of practical leadership applications.

What makes this book especially meaningful is its focus on the individual as leader. It is not so much a focus on leadership skills alone but instead centers more on the person of the leader and the expression of the role as a manifestation of who the leader is rather than simply what the leader does. While most leadership texts focus on the skills and talents associated with good leadership, this book expresses leadership as a vehicle for personal growth, relationship building, and impacting the lives of others.

A strength of this text is its use of real-time situations and scenarios which serve as a forum for the opportunities and applications of leadership. These real stories of leadership reveal and visualize actual experiences that help frame the requisites of leadership and allow the reader to reflect on how these applications can be internalized. From these examples, leaders can translate the suggested applications into his or her personal experience and model them in personal roles.

Nancy attempts to further personalize leadership by making a real connection to the reader. Rather than instructing, Nancy engages readers in a way that *invests* them. She brings them into the actual experiences of leadership. Almost from within the pages, she invites participation in the learning through identification with the issues and applications so directly that personally applying these principles seems a natural extension of reading about them.

What I find especially satisfying about this leadership book is how much I sense the words and thoughts about leadership as a reflection of Nancy herself. In so many ways, this book is an expression of her leadership capacity, sensitivity, connection, and expression. Her ability to be fully present and to model sound leadership attributes bore much fruit judging from the many accomplishments and successes across the full of her career. I am not alone in recognizing that Nancy's special leadership gifts helped both people and organizations, especially exemplified by the dramatic success of Sigma Theta Tau International during Nancy's tenure. Readers should do no less in developing their own leadership capacity. For that they can expect no less than the personal and professional success Nancy attained through her own exemplary leadership. Learning from this book will help make that success more possible.

Tim Porter-O'Grady, DM, EdD, APRN, FAAN
Senior Partner and Mediator
Tim Porter-O'Grady Associates, Inc.
Atlanta, Georgia, USA
Associate Professor and Leadership Scholar
College of Nursing and Healthcare Innovation
Arizona State University, Phoenix, Arizona, USA

Preface

*For the purposes of this book, leadership is defined as making
a difference for others by using the gift of yourself, having clarity
of vision, displaying passion and trust, valuing others,
and creating environments for effective action.*

Ideas for a book arise from many sources. This one comes from a request to share previous writings with a broader audience; from the desire to share years of research, learning, and experience in leadership with others; and from an annoyance that many people confuse leadership with management.

While the two concepts and disciplines of leadership and management certainly overlap and interact with one another in practice, they are indeed separate and distinct. What strikes me most about their distinctness is how it is exhibited behaviorally. For example, managers administer and maintain, while leaders innovate and create; managers focus on the here, now, and how, while leaders focus on the future, long range, and why; and managers do things right while leaders do the right thing (Bennis, 2003).

Other things that strike me about the differences are the journey and learning required for an individual to achieve leadership or management excellence. For the manager, the journey frequently involves learning and practicing technical skills. For example, a great manager can effectively and efficiently manage projects, monitor financial objectives, establish and meet outcome measures, and organize and coordinate activities. The journey for a leader, on the other hand, involves learning and practicing adaptive skills. Great leaders effectively create environments and cultures that inspire, motivate, and empower people; provide a guiding vision for what can be; exhibit a passion and appreciation for the work at hand, even in the face of obstacles or failure; and display self-awareness and courage while taking risks and challenging others for the greater good.

The result of leader and manager journeys, while distinct, are both critical to the success of organizations, institutions, and communities. One cannot exist without the other. Imagine a community or institution that has doers but no guiding vision, or a dreamer who has no followers to enact the dream. There would be only inertia, unproductive resistance to change.

Managers would maintain the status quo, and leaders would innovate without implementation. The world needs both—great managers and great leaders working together to achieve visions, goals, tasks, and outcomes.

Research and experience have taught me this. I also learned that it's nearly impossible for a person to be a great leader and a great manager at the same time. This is not to say that some managers do not have or display leadership characteristics, or that some leaders are not well-versed in the art and science of managing. Nor does it mean that managers cannot journey on to become leaders, or that leaders who have been managers cannot effectively return to management. What it does say is, for people to stay true to the paths they have chosen for their lives, they must avoid the distractions of other paths to focus on the one they have chosen.

If a person focuses on the management path, he or she will engage in training and experiences that are deductive, static, factual, goal-oriented, reactive, short-term, rule-oriented, predictive, and guided by common sense. Those who choose to be leaders focus on dynamics, exploration and discovery, risk, self-knowledge, ideas, change, flexibility, and long-range perspective (Bennis, 2003). The strengths individuals develop to become effective leaders or managers are different and require full attention if they are to be mastered successfully.

In this book, I focus on the journey of leadership, with journey defined as the continual movement and evolution of a person from one place to another throughout life. The journey of management will be left to another author. I will concentrate on the adaptive characteristics of a leader—identifying them, illustrating them through stories, and challenging readers to assess their own characteristics and readiness to step onto the leadership path.

For the latter, a journal or notebook might be particularly helpful as you will have an opportunity to develop your personal leadership development plan along the way. Volumes have been written on each of these adaptive leadership characteristics. My goal in this book is to provide starter ideas for developing or expanding those characteristics for you.

For the purposes of this book, leadership is defined as making a difference for others by using the gift of you, having clarity of vision, displaying passion and trust, valuing others, and creating environments for effective action.

I wish you success on your leadership journey and Godspeed.

—*Nancy Dickenson-Hazard*

Part I

Being Ready

Leaders come in all shapes and sizes with all manner of styles and strengths. For some, becoming a leader is a natural progression of their career; for others, it is the result of random opportunities. For all, it is a lifelong journey that necessitates continual learning, self-awareness, and growth.

For the wise, leadership requires a deliberate thoroughness of preparation to be ready to meet and carry out the leadership challenge at hand. Being ready to lead obliges the individual to truthfully answer questions of ability, commitment, and intellect. This high level of self-discovery is essential to effective, meaningful, and influential leadership.

Chapter 1

I Believe Therefore I Am:
Being Purpose- and Values-Driven

All leadership journeys require self-examination, knowledge, perseverance, and courage.

- Self-examination, so you are comfortable with who you are and what you stand for.

- Knowledge of your passion or what drives and energizes you.

- Perseverance in developing, expanding, refining, and using your competency and skill.

- Courage to challenge, change, act, speak, and do.

Leaders must be in command of themselves before they can command and lead others. Clarifying purpose and values is the first step on the leadership journey.

To illustrate the importance of defining purpose and owning values, Peter Drucker, an author best known for his principles on managing by objectives, wrote an essay titled "Not Enough Generals Were Killed" (Drucker, 1996). He observes in this essay that leaders are not preachers, but rather *doers* with conviction. He tells a story from his high school years when his history teacher assigned each student a book to read on World War I. After carefully reading the historical accounts, each student was to write and present an essay for discussion. During one of these discussions, a classmate of Peter's observed that every one of the assigned books said that the Great War was one of military incompetence, and he inquired of his teacher why that was. The teacher, who had served and was injured in that war, did not hesitate to answer, "Because not enough generals were killed; they stayed way behind the lines and let others do the fighting and dying" (p. xiv).

Years later, Drucker's education and leadership experiences made clear to him what the teacher meant: Effective leaders, while they do and must delegate, never relinquish the only thing that will make a difference and set the standard—their own sense of purpose and value. Leaders do what it takes to accomplish their purpose. The generals in World War I, while knowledgeable in tactics, did not display or convey a sense of purpose by leading and joining their men in battle. In the teacher's opinion, they chose to play it safe. By not being with their men, they conveyed that they did not value defending their country.

 ## Purposeful Vision

Sally, a nurse practitioner, worked in pediatrics in a mid-size, urban health maintenance organization with five pediatricians and two other nurse practitioners. Sally was the most adamant of all of them about the importance of promoting health through education, with a focus on growth and development, nutrition, behavior modification, caring for minor acute illnesses like colds, and effective child-rearing practices. She spent the majority of her allotted 20-minute visits with patients and parents promoting health and preventing illness, while her colleagues were more interested in seeing patients who were sicker and presented more complex cases.

Sally strongly valued the well-being of others and doing the right thing for her patients, teaching and offering guidance and resources to promote their health. She firmly believed that her greatest strength as a health care provider was keeping children well, and she felt there was not enough emphasis on preventive care in that health maintenance organization.

Her idea was simple. Use two hours a week out of the nurse practitioner's schedule to do two things: First, make phone calls to at-risk, first-time parents to assess and prevent problems; and second, hold weekly parenting sessions to discuss normal newborn and infant behaviors so parents would be better prepared to cope when they occurred.

Resistance by administration was high; two hours a week was six patients not seen and not billed! But Sally was persistent. Armed with research and data, she repeatedly presented her case. She even volunteered time in the evening to hold the classes. She also garnered support from her care-provider colleagues.

After several months of pursuing her goal, Sally was granted six months to implement a pilot program to test her proposal. The results? Phone calls into the office for new-parent advice were reduced by 10% because the parents were receiving proactive advice and the incoming parental calls were more likely to be for legitimate problems rather than for non-acute issues or reassurance. Moreover, those who attended the filled-to-capacity classes were less likely to use emergency services for problems such as colic or teething. The results impressed Sally's colleagues and administrators. Twenty years later, the program is still in place, but now *daily* allocations of time are allotted for parent training. The classes also continue but have been expanded to three times a week, and a class for parents of toddlers has been added.

Sally had a purpose she vigorously pursued that made a difference for her patients, their families, and her employer. Most of all, she made a difference for herself by not letting go of what she believed in.

Purpose, Values, and Talents

PURPOSE

Purpose is the result you want to create. It is the impact you wish to leave behind, what you work toward, and what you want to be remembered for—it is where your values and talents make a solid connection to everyday actions.

VALUES

Values are closely aligned with purpose and are the qualities and standards regarded as valuable, important, and worthy of esteem.

TALENTS

Talents are our natural abilities that, when used, generate energy and are intrinsically rewarding to us. They are vehicles for expressing our values on the way to fulfilling our purpose.

Purpose

Purpose is the result you want to create. It is the impact you wish to leave behind, what you work toward, and what you want to be remembered for—it is where your values and talents make a solid connection to everyday actions. Being purpose-driven brings meaningful significance and fulfillment to your life and work. It requires energy and unwavering commitment to constant renewal.

Values

"You are free to be yourself when you are cognizant of your values and talents."

Values are closely aligned with purpose and are the qualities and standards regarded as valuable, important, and worthy of esteem. Values can be tangible or intangible. For example, we value food, clothing, and shelter, but we might also value trust, respect, and honesty. Whatever values we have, certain ones govern our lives and are core to making us who we are. They motivate, drive, and dictate our actions as we move toward the impact or purpose we are pursuing. Core values give us energy and center our purpose. They are qualities we freely cherish, willingly affirm publicly, and act on regularly (Klein, 2006).

Talents

Talents are our natural abilities that, when used, generate energy and are intrinsically rewarding to us. They are vehicles for expressing our values on the way to fulfilling our purpose. Talents are fundamental to who we are and their use makes our lives and work more significant and meaningful.

"Often, positive or high experiences are those in which you were using your talents, your values were aligned with the organization and people you were working with, and you were actively contributing to the shared goal of the group."

 ## Connecting to Purpose, Values, and Talents

The importance of being in touch with our values and talents and being purpose-centered came home to me when my daughter, recently graduated from university, began her own journey toward leadership. She began looking for a job and was struggling with many life choices: Where should she live? Should she move first or get the job first? What kind of job did she want? What about the future—graduate school, progressive career, fulfilling her personal life?

To me, the world was her oyster and she could create whatever she wanted and whatever would bring fulfillment. To her, her life was full of distressing chaos. One day, in a state of near-hysteria, she listed five issues that were weighing heavily on her mind. It became clear to me that she was indeed spinning her wheels and would not find solid ground without some clarity of purpose. So I asked her, "Do you want to solve these little problems or deal with the bigger issue of purpose?"

Her immediate reaction was hostility and frustration because I had called her problems "little," but after a while she calmed down and asked what I meant. I suggested that she would always encounter problems in life and that they would never go away but just return in different forms. She could choose to be reactive in solving problems as they came up or she could take time to connect with her values and talents and decide what kind of impact she wanted to make in her professional life and proactively pursue that.

We talked about not being creatures of our circumstances but rather creating circumstances by clarifying our values and talents. We discussed turning negatives into positives by understanding our basic purpose and centering our emotions and actions on that purpose. In the process, we come to a better realization of our worth and potential contributions.

After several more days of chaos and hand-wringing, she concluded my suggestions would help, and we set off on a half-day adventure of value identification, talent naming, life purpose statements, and readiness assessments. At the end of the day, she said her head hurt from all the self-discovery! Several weeks later, while visiting her in her new city and home, she told me she had learned so much from that afternoon. "It has really helped me on my job interviews and to see what companies and jobs I would be good at. I know what I am looking for now and don't want to settle for less." She had truly moved from organized chaos to purposeful, value-driven proactivity and within two weeks was starting work at her "awesome" first job.

You are free to be yourself when you are cognizant of your values and talents. You will act and behave in a manner consistent with who you are and what you believe. When values and talents are given voice through your defined purpose, you are more fulfilled and more engaged in your life and work, and you become a leader who is making a difference.

Readiness and Reflection

1. Readiness Query*

   Determine your readiness to embark on or advance your leadership journey by answering "yes" or "no" to the following statements.

   _____ I want to build my personal leadership abilities.

   _____ I am clear as to *why* I want to develop my leadership abilities.

   _____ I am willing to devote regular time and energy to my personal leadership development.

   _____ I am willing to change behavior and thinking to achieve my leadership goals.

   _____ I am open to adopting new approaches.

   _____ I have the support I need to develop personal leadership skills.

   _____ I am confident of my leadership potential.

   _____ I believe in continual self-discovery.

   Reflect on your answers, particularly the "no" responses. Ask yourself what you need to do to make these statements true. Consider what you might do to transition from a negative or reactive response to a positive or proactive response. Record your responses in a journal.

   *Adapted from: Prism Ltd. (n.d.). *Community leadership programs.* Retrieved July 25 2008, from http://www.prismltd.com/leader.htm and from Quinn, R.E. (2004). *Building the bridge as you walk on it.* New Jersey: Jossey-Bass, John Wiley & Sons.

2. Experiential Highs and Lows

   On a sheet of paper, make three columns. Label the first column "The Highs," the second column "The Lows," and the third "Characteristics." Now, reflect on past professional experiences and record in the "Highs" column those experiences that evoke a positive memory. Record in the "Lows" column experiences that left you with a dissatisfying or negative memory. Reflect on each experience. Then, in the "Characteristics" column, respond to the following questions:

- What was I doing that made the experience negative or positive?

- Who was I doing it with?

- What outcomes made the experience negative or positive?

Once your chart is complete, look closely at the characteristics for your "High" experiences and identify similarities. Do the same for the "Low" ones. Frequently, upon completing this exercise, people see patterns that provide insight into the type of activities, relationships, and outcomes of an experience that have contributed to negative or positive feelings. Often, positive or high experiences are those in which you were using your talents, your values were aligned with the organization and people you were working with, and you were actively contributing to the shared goal of the group. Conversely, the negative or low experiences are just the opposite. Being more aware of your core values and talents will only heighten your professional experiences and increase your sense of contribution and worth.

3. Values and Talents Assessment

On a sheet of paper, make two columns. Label one "Values" and the other "Talents." Keep in mind that a value is a quality or principle that you regard as desirable and important to you, such as creativity, honesty, learning, or trust. Talents are natural abilities that give you energy and are fulfilling when used, such as writing, researching, talking with and listening to people, or analyzing information. Write in the "Values" column 10 values you hold dear and consider essential to your life. In the "Talents" column, list 10 talents or strengths you consider essential to your being.

Reflect on the values and talents you have written and place an asterisk by the five values and five talents you consider most important. Ask yourself the following question: *Why are these particular values and talents so important to me?* Jot your thoughts down beside the value or talent.

Now, do two more development exercises. First, return to your "Highs and Lows" chart and reflect on which of your core values and talents were met and used in circumstances that were highly gratifying, and which of your values and talents were used in situations that were emotionally dissatisfying. As pointed out previously, times of high gratification occur when your values are honored and your talents are being used, and low gratification occurs when they are not.

"With increased self-awareness comes increased authenticity—a life that is based on and aligned with principles, beliefs, and what you do best."

Second, have a conversation about your values and talents with a trusted confidant. Remember, for a value to be a core value, it must be publicly claimed and used freely. Your conversation with your confidant should center around two questions: 1) How do you see these values and talents in my actions? 2) What do you suggest I do to maximize alignment and use of my values and talents in my work and life?

Reflections and conversations such as these not only validate your own value and talent identification, they also enhance further discovery about yourself as to how well you live out your values and use your talents. Another benefit of this exercise is that it helps you identify other values and talents you may not be aware of. With increased self-awareness comes increased authenticity—a life that is based on and aligned with principles, beliefs, and what you do best.

4. Purpose Statement and Life Story

Describe in one sentence your life's purpose. Some experts call this your legacy statement, others your personal mission statement. Still others call it a life statement. Regardless of the term, in writing this statement, focus on several elements: 1) What impact or result do I want to have? 2) What do I want to be remembered for? 3) What will I use and what values will I express to achieve this? When constructing this statement, it is helpful to consider filling in the blanks for the following: I will create (impact) by expressing (values) by using (talents).

A sample purpose statement might read, "I will stimulate professionals to realize their full leadership potential by mentoring, interacting, and communicating with them with integrity, intelligence, and caring." The objective of purpose statements is to daily remind yourself of the impact you wish to have and to help you remember that, to achieve this impact, it is vitally important to align your actions with your values and use your talents as actions.

Writing your life story engages you in designing circumstances around which your purpose will take place. When writing the story, consider not only what you are doing and where it is happening, but also where you are living, what you look like, and what your relationships are. The life story gives you license to dream and describe your world and your life in as much detail as you wish. Stories do need to be realistic, however, and demonstrate balance between what you are striving for and what your circumstances allow. If stories are to serve as motivators for achieving the difference you want to make and the impact you want to achieve, they need to align and be consistent with what you believe, what you have to offer, and what steps can realistically be taken to reach your purpose.

5. Reflect on what you have discovered about yourself, your purpose, and your values from this chapter and the exercises.

   Write one paragraph about where you see yourself today.

6. Begin your personal leadership development plan.

   Develop two strategies to improve identification and alignment of your purpose and values. Start your plan by writing these down.

Chapter 2

Whose Life Is It, Anyway? Being Authentic

Authenticity is the state of being genuine, where there is alignment of what is said, done, and displayed. It means sacrificing self-focus for the greater goal of opening oneself to external forces and creating new patterns of being rather than accepting the status quo. Authenticity has been termed by some as "ego death," for it demands seeing things impersonally at all times, facing everything and avoiding nothing, taking unconditional responsibility for oneself, and standing alone, living fearlessly (Cohen, 2008).

Authenticity is not an easy state to reach, but it is the very foundation of leadership. In the final analysis, leadership is really an expression of who we are and what we believe. To create value and significance, the leader must be real, genuine, authentic, encouraging, and empowering of others to be the same.

> "Leadership is really an expression of who we are and what we believe."

There is no greater satisfaction than leading a group of people to accomplish a worthy goal while observing their talents and authenticity unfold. Given this, everyone has the chance to be a leader. It is not the title, the power, the style, or the image that makes a person a leader. It is being true and genuine to purpose and values, along with the willingness to act on it that makes a person a leader.

Authenticity is rooted in acute self-awareness, discipline, and adherence to living by values with confidence in self and others.

Self-Awareness and Self-Discipline

Awareness comes not only from being in touch with values and talents but, perhaps more importantly, gaining significance through willingness to take the risk of questioning yourself and being open to external input. You become open to higher levels of discovery, awareness, and competence when you go outside your comfort zone, asking for and listening to different perspectives, and shift from "How can I fix this?" to the more receptive mind-set of "What does this tell me about my behavior that I can change so it is more reflective of my values?"

The power of mind-set should not be underestimated in the quest for greater self-awareness. Mind-sets are models of how we believe the world around us works or is supposed to work. In some ways, mind-sets are tunnel vision. They structure the way we see and think about things from a narrow frame of reference, based on our internal analysis and experiences. Deeply ingrained, these perceptions operate invisibly and drive what we do and how we do it, whether accurate or not.

A receptive mind-set is one that keeps the larger purpose in the forefront. It uses knowledge, values, points of view, and experiences from a multitude of sources and aligns them with personal and work values. A receptive mind-set creates an environment where the individual can question, listen, express, appreciate, and serve through awareness and authenticity.

 Self-Awareness Journey

Joyce accepted a newly created senior leadership position in a large health-care company. She was hired not only for her previous experience in administration, but also for her nursing expertise, as the company wanted to improve nursing satisfaction and retention. They felt a nurse could best relate to the needs of other nurses and wanted to fill the position with someone respected in the field.

Joyce fit the bill. She reported directly to the chief executive and was responsible for overseeing all of the company's administrative functions, including human resources. It was a definite step up. She came to the position with many managerial skills, but her personal leadership journey and experiences were less developed. She strongly desired to serve the company mission and placed high value on collaboration, accountability, and teamwork. Her actions, however, led others to question her sincerity.

Joyce would lead a team meeting in an open dialogue approach, acknowledging members' contributions to the goals and mission of the company. She planned group team-building activities and carefully sought input from each participant during strategic planning sessions. However, she often criticized, dictated, and micromanaged employees during individual meetings, leading many of her subordinates to question her sincerity. They also questioned whether she was really interested in advancing nursing within the company.

After awhile, when it became apparent that her colleagues were avoiding her and, at times, working at cross-purposes, Joyce began feeling marginalized. One day, she solicited feedback from a colleague who honestly shared perceptions and beliefs of the group about her behavior. At first angry, and then downright depressed, Joyce went to a trusted confidante. After many conversations and a great deal of introspection, she recognized that the source of her problem was her fear of failure and her mind-set—fueled by previous experiences—that she had to directly control all activities that impinged on outcomes for which she was directly responsible.

Her awareness journey eventually led her to believe that each person has a valuable contribution to make and, if she was to gain the respect and trust she valued, other people needed to be empowered and trusted. She realized that, given their own awareness and knowledge, people make the best choices they can. By providing her colleagues with resources and encouragement, she could facilitate the best choices possible for the company.

Joyce became aware that each person has his or her own internal resources, and that she was responsible for her own satisfaction, happiness, and results. Her path toward self-awareness was rocky and sometimes difficult but in the end she replaced her fear of failure with determination to learn from failure and her impulse to control others with a passion to empower them. Her self-awareness led to the company's best-ever year for nurse retention and satisfaction.

By opening up to herself, Joyce became more open with others. The previous atmosphere of doubt was replaced by trust and collaboration. She has continued to make self-discoveries and is truly becoming a purpose-driven, authentic leader.

Live According to Your Values

> *"To be an authentic leader, the only choice is to live according to your values."*

According to conventional wisdom, decisions and actions are easier if a person lives according to his or her values. Decisions and actions might be clearer when a person lives according to his or her values, but they by no means are always easy. Values are the pavement, or basis, for what we do and how we do it. They are what we walk on and live by. Frequently, we are presented with circumstances and events that counter our values. The co-worker who wants to cut corners just to get the job done might counter another staff member's value of caring about the quality of the organization's work. The boss who berates subordinates in front of others might assail a person's values of compassion and understanding. Or, a co-worker who stretches the truth to place him- or herself in a better light might counter a colleague's values of integrity, honesty, and trust.

Daily, we are confronted with moral and ethical decisions and situations that require us to live out or ignore our values. *We have the choice of allowing circumstances to control us or being a catalyst for change by expressing and acting on our values.* Sometimes those choices are easy, and sometimes they are not. But, to be an authentic leader, the only choice is to live according to your values.

Searching Deep

Andrew had been on the job for six months and was advancing quite well in his competency and skill. His performance evaluations were positive, and he was feeling more competent and knowledgeable each day. He was quickly learning the ropes—the way things got done in that medical center's emergency department culture.

Some of what he observed, such as the proficiency and efficiency of the staff, he admired and tried to emulate. Other behaviors troubled him, particularly the practice of putting indigent, uninsured patients at the end of the waiting list and moving them further down the list as new patients came in. This happened whether the new patient had an emergency or not. The practice, which was particularly true on busy nights, was changed only when life-threatening conditions demanded. It was not unusual for an uninsured patient who had a broken or displaced limb, moderate respiratory discomfort, or a wound requiring suturing to wait for hours.

Andrew had chosen to work in this hospital because of its service-minded mission. It had appealed to his values of caring, compassion, and service to others, but there was little evidence of these values in action. Daily, he watched people in pain wait for treatment and caregivers too harried to help.

One evening, a mother brought in a young boy who had what appeared to be a compound leg fracture. The boy was in a great deal of pain, and the mother was naturally distraught. Andrew's compassion and need to care for them took over, and he brought them back to an examination room to implement the protocol for a broken limb.

As he was caring for the boy, Andrew's supervisor interrupted, calling him out of the room. In a calm, matter-of-fact tone, she informed him that this patient was not the priority and that he should care for another less acutely ill person who had just come in. He tried to reason with the supervisor that this patient needed help before the one waiting, but he was overruled. Rather than risk retribution, he complied. Later, he learned that the boy and his mother were uninsured. While the boy eventually received care, it was given grudgingly.

Andrew felt terrible. He was discouraged about his ability to stand up for the little boy and disappointed that he had not lived up to his own values and beliefs. It was a hard blow to realize this. For days, Andrew had an increasingly hard time working in an environment that did not live up to the organization's stated mission and diminished his own sense of self-worth. Eventually, Andrew left this hospital because he could no longer compromise what he valued and believed. The next time he searched for a job, he looked for one where the belief system was evident in behaviors and actions displayed throughout the organization and were aligned with his own.

We usually deal with difficult experiences in one of two ways: We become angry and lash out or we withdraw and stop trying. A third option, however, is to have faith and learn from the situation—to keep moving on even though we are not exactly sure where that will lead us (Quinn, 2004). Learning occurs when we move on, reflect on the circumstance, and rely on values to guide us. We learn how to think, behave, and live differently. In doing so, we positively alter our lives and the lives of those around us.

Confidence in Self and Others

Confidence is belief in ability and worth. Leaders demonstrate confidence in themselves; they possess self-worth because they know who they are and what they stand for. Through introspection, dialogue with others, and experience, they have a keen sense of what they bring to a situation and the difference they can make. Because of this confidence, they are willing to go into uncertain situations to pursue their higher purpose, learning and adapting as they traverse the terrain to fulfill that purpose.

Achieving confidence is a nimble balancing act that requires leaders to constantly take stock of behaviors and recognize that other people are equal to them in value. Leaders must be willing not only to credit others for successes but also join them in accepting responsibility for failures.

Readiness and Reflection

1. Reflect on your current authenticity. Write a paragraph describing yourself, and include the assets that make you authentic.

2. Check each characteristic you believe you possess:

   _____ Clarity of purpose

   _____ Live by values

   _____ Self-awareness

   _____ Self-discipline

   _____ Self-confidence

   _____ Adaptability

   _____ Flexible in action, reaction, and proaction

   _____ Confident in others

   _____ Have a greater purpose than myself

   _____ Ability to deal with change and uncertainty

   _____ Welcome and learn from failure

   _____ Transform awareness into creative action

3. Reflect on the list and the characteristics you checked and write a paragraph that describes your assets of authenticity—as you want them to be—and what you will do to develop them.

4. List events you have seen or been a part of where you have observed a person in the role of a change catalyst, versus a change controller. What behaviors did you see or experience in those circumstances?

5. Make a list of things you do well. Ask a friend, colleague, or mentor to make a similar list. Compare and reflect on the similarities and differences and discuss for clarity.

6. Make a list of your top five priority values. Next to each value, identify one or two actions that you will take to live by that value.

7. Reflect on what you have learned from this chapter and these exercises. Write a paragraph on where you see yourself today as an authentic leader.

8. Develop two strategies for improving your authenticity, and add them to your personal leadership development plan.

Chapter 3

Whose Life Is It, Anyway?
Being Trustworthy

People are fickle, and trust is fragile. As a leader, if you have trust, you can move mountains; without it, there is inertia at best, disintegration at worst. Because trust is so fragile, it is one of the most important things to cultivate and maintain. It is the glue that binds people together.

Trust provides a leader with legitimacy and credibility, and true leaders value it as the common bond to achieve greater purpose. Leaders constantly strive to be trustworthy, to model trusting behaviors, and to expect trustworthiness in their followers.

> *"Because trust is so fragile, it is one of the most important things to cultivate and maintain. It is the glue that binds people together."*

Trust is belief and confidence in the honesty and integrity of one's self and others. It implies being open and able to listen, to speak the truth. Trusting someone means suspending judgment and following through, delivering what is promised. A trusting leader believes in the talents of others and carefully takes in their ideas, knowing that they may potentially be better than his or her own ideas.

Trusting leaders do not shut out ideas, mind-sets, and mental models from others, nor do they fail to keep promises. They work and thrive in an atmosphere of sincerity and candor because, to succeed, they must be open to alternatives and innovation. Trusting leaders operate with truth and integrity.

 ## The Power of Trust

Sue, the nurse manager of a heart catheterization lab in a community hospital, encountered a 60-year-old woman who was prepared for the procedure but still distraught as she worried that something would go wrong. Despite repeated assurances by the assigned assistant, the woman was not comforted. The assistant sought help from Sue.

What Sue did was a form of low-tech magic: she merely cleared the room of people, dimmed the lights, sat down beside the woman, and listened. Taking the woman's hand, Sue asked what aspect of the procedure was so frightening to her. Sue sat and listened to the woman's story about a friend who had undergone the same procedure and experienced complications, and the woman just knew the same would happen to her.

Sue talked to the woman about her fears. She gave legitimacy to them and showed concern. Detailing her knowledge about the procedures and the precautions taken to avoid complications, she reassured the woman she would be there to take care of and watch over her. They talked for at least 20 minutes before the assistant returned to take the woman to the procedure room. Sue walked with her, holding her hand and getting her to talk about her family. As the woman was situated on the procedure table, she acknowledged her fear and, in a joking tone, told the other caregivers that she was not sure if she trusted them, but she did trust Sue, so she'd be all right.

Trust is powerful; it can overcome fear, give confidence, ease doubt, and move people to do things they never imagined. Trust is the cornerstone of great leadership.

Integrity

Integrity is the basis for truth and trust. It goes beyond basic truth telling, as it is total congruence between who we are (values) and what we do (actions). When a leader aligns words and behavior with values, trust is the outcome. To be effective, leaders must have integrity and be worthy of the trust placed in them. Without integrity, there is no credibility for the leader, and without credibility, there is no relationship, communication, or movement toward the greater goal. Integrity affects everything the leader does, says, and influences.

> *"When a leader aligns words and behavior with values, trust is the outcome."*

Integrity is the centerpiece of leadership, the beginning and end of a journey. Studies have repeatedly demonstrated that integrity is the number one leadership characteristic considered essential by those who follow (Kouzes & Posner, 2006, 2007). This consistent finding is the result of followers' beliefs that the degree of leader integrity reflects on followers' individual and collective integrity.

People seek to follow someone who does as he or she professes and behaves with principle, so that association with that leader does not reflect badly on them as individuals. Hence, followers value a leader who continually moves toward increasing levels of integrity, both personally and collectively, and they take note when there is consistency between word and deed.

> *"Integrity is the basis for truth and trust."*

Leaders who live and act with integrity have a profound effect on those around them. The more a leader develops and displays integrity, the more those who work with the leader and the organization they serve demonstrate integrity. Integrity begets integrity. It creates honest interaction and trueness to values, principles, and beliefs, along with recognition of and adjustment to the ever-changing reality of an organization's environment.

Most of us spend our entire lives defining and refining our integrity and behaving in a manner that models this. It is difficult to stick to values when a different path appears easier or more advantageous, but leaders with integrity become role models and an inspiration to others, creating a value-driven team, workforce, and organization.

"Integrity begets integrity."

 ## Living Out Values at Chick-fil-A

S. Truett Cathy is the founder of Chick-fil-A, which currently operates more than 1,300 restaurants in the United States. When customers go to Chick-fil-A for its chicken fare, they enter a place where work philosophy and values are strongly spiritual and Christian.

Ever since the company's first restaurant opened in 1946, Chick-fil-A has been closed on Sundays to allow employees and customers a day of spirituality. Despite the practice of competitors having Sunday hours that potentially reap higher financial yields, Cathy stuck to his belief and kept his restaurants closed.

Here is what has happened:

1. Cathy's integrity has become well-known and admired. Other businesses such as Intel, Hobby Lobby, and subsidiaries of Wal-Mart now offer employee-based spiritual services, and some even close their doors on Sunday.

2. Chick-fil-A has one of the most committed workforces in the fast-food industry. Commitment improves business relationships and productivity and also reduces turnover.

3. The chain has recorded 40 consecutive years of annual sales increases and did $2.64 billion in business in 2007, a 16% increase from the previous year, discounting the premise that not being open on Sunday hurts business.

The man who coined the phrase "Eat Mor Chikin: Inspire More People" exemplifies how a person who aligned values with actions has influenced business, workers, and people in general (Cathy, 2002).

Readiness and Reflection

1. Integrity assessment. Reflect on your 10 dominant values and write down two actions, decisions, or behaviors for each that demonstrate cohesion between who you are (values) and what you do (actions).

2. Identify from the list of characteristics below which ones you wish to improve.

   _____ I am dependable.

   _____ I am open and honest in my communication with others.

   _____ I listen carefully to what others say.

   _____ I regularly think about how I can better align my behavior with my values.

   _____ I am honest with others and myself, even if it is difficult.

   _____ I put the interest of others before myself.

   _____ I believe in and maintain high standards in my work.

   _____ I am reliable and follow through on what I say I will do.

   _____ I have a high work ethic for myself.

   Every day, select a characteristic you would like to improve and write down two things you will do. Go through the list and concentrate on a new characteristic each day, repeating them as needed.

3. Reflect on a situation in which you feel your trust was violated. Describe how you felt, how you reacted, and what you would do differently should a similar situation occur in the future. Identify the personal value you feel was challenged.

4. Secure a mission and values (or principles) statement from your employer, and read it over carefully. If there are elements you do not fully understand, discuss them with your supervisor or colleagues. After the discussion, reflect on and record your responses to the following questions:

    a. What are the organization's expressed values?

    b. How do I experience those values in my employment?

    c. What are my priority values?

    d. Do I see alignment between my values and the organization's values?

5. Where there is not congruence or alignment between your values and your organization's values, write down what you will do to resolve this conflict.

6. Reflect on what you have read and the exercises you have completed. Write a paragraph about where you see yourself today as a trustworthy leader.

7. Develop two strategies for improving your trustworthiness, and add them to your personal leadership development plan.

Chapter 4

My Energy Flows: Being Passionate

All of us are driven to act by internal and external forces—internal forces such as a desire, need, or will and external forces such as rewards, praise, or money. For leaders, the most powerful forces are internal. These forces keep leaders going despite naysayers, criticism or failures. These internal forces are powerful, because they give meaning and fulfillment to the leader's life. From the leader's perspective, a primary reason to engage in an activity or be involved in an organization is to pursue purpose and impact greater than self. This strong desire to pursue what is more meaningful than self is passion.

Have you ever felt so strongly about something that you were driven to do something about it? Take Rosa Parks, for example, who felt so strongly about the inequity of not being allowed to sit in the front of the bus because of the color of her skin. Parks' passion for equality sparked a national civil rights debate and caused the people of the United States to examine their values.

"These ordinary people with ordinary lives had a fire inside, a cause that motivated them to action. They had passion."

Or think about the nurse from Portland, Oregon, who felt such compassion for homeless people in her community that she gave up her full-time job, solicited donations of goods and money, sought out professional colleagues to volunteer time, and established a nurse-managed health clinic. Her passion led to provision of primary care for hundreds of homeless people and sparked national interest in replicating such health centers.

Then there's the 12-year-old girl whose leukemia was in remission. She wanted to provide comfort for other children experiencing some of the same treatments she had undergone. She started a teddy-bear drive for her local children's hospital and gave teddy bears to hundreds of children with cancer. Teddy-bear drives are now commonplace in most children's hospitals. These ordinary people with ordinary lives had a fire inside, a cause that motivated them to action. They had passion.

Drive Versus Passion

This kind of commitment beyond self is not rare; in fact, we all have the opportunity to feel and express it. The challenge is to activate it. As Bennis (2003) points out, everyone is born with passion for life, but somewhere along life's journey, that passion or desire to make things happen for a greater good gets confused with drive, or having to constantly prove ourselves. Drive by itself is callous and deadly; but when married to desire or passion, drive is rewarding and effective.

 Pursuing Your Passion

Terry was a floating nurse in a suburban hospital. While certain aspects of his job were appealing, such as learning new skills and meeting new people, floating did not allow Terry to develop relationships with patients, families, and colleagues, the part of the nursing role that he truly valued. He felt quite passionate about continuity of care and being able to follow patients all the way through their hospitalization. Floating only gave him a glimpse. Terry also felt he was meant to be an educator and had a strong desire to contribute to the profession in this way, but there was little opportunity to do that in his current job.

Terry had an analytical mind, enjoyed helping people learn, and felt energized by intellectual discussion and debate. He was constantly sharing with colleagues new pieces of information and knowledge that he thought would improve practice, and he took pride when someone "got it" and tried it in their work. He firmly believed in using evidence in his practice and, when working with someone, would always talk through what he was doing and why, based on research. In sum, Terry enjoyed learning and imparting knowledge to others.

Every day, Terry went to work floating from floor to floor, doing his job, driven by his paycheck. He was just doing a job. Many days, he went home drained, and not at all sure of the impact he had made on his patients. He would tell himself to be grateful—he had a job and was amassing all sorts of experience that would serve him in the future.

After one particularly trying day, however, Terry said enough is enough! He was not happy with what he was doing and decided to pursue what he felt passionate about. He set a plan in motion to pursue graduate studies while still working, but as a clinical instructor, a preceptor. This change made Terry come alive. Despite the fact that he was working and going to school, he was more fulfilled and more energetic because he was pursuing his passion.

Enthusiasm, Energy, Determination

Passion, in addition to being fueled by a desire to make things happen for a larger good, is frequently characterized by enthusiasm, energy and determination. I was once told that I was not college material and later was informed that I'd never get into graduate school. In response to these assessments, I was driven by a desire to demonstrate that my intellect was worthy of development and that, with the right opportunities, I could make a significant difference to my chosen profession of nursing.

I was determined not to just bring home a paycheck, but to influence the health and lives of my patients. As my passion grew to influence the health of people through the art and science of nursing, opportunities to express and live out this passion emerged. I never set out to be the leader of an international nursing organization founded on knowledge and leadership principles; my passion and congruency of values delivered me there.

Passion is infectious. When people witness a leader who is enthusiastic, bounding with energy because he or she feels strongly about an issue, cause or organization, it is hard to turn away. Any project or organization is only as strong and effective in influencing its cause as the people who are engaged with it. If the leader is weak in conviction and commitment, those working with that leader follow suit. However, if leaders are genuinely passionate about what is being done and for whom it is done, others will catch their fervor.

"Passion, in addition to being fueled by a desire to make things happen for a larger good, is frequently characterized by enthusiasm, energy and determination."

Leaders are constantly looking for people to embrace passion with them. They seek people to do the work of making a difference *with* them, not *for* them. They believe firmly in the power of many and steer away from the authority of one. To do this, leaders continually examine what they do and measure their achievement in terms of collective effort and values fulfillment. Daily, leaders look in the mirror to make sure the person they see is the kind of person they want to be—a person they respect and believe in.

Leaders have an obligation to never let go of their passion and their commitment. They do the work of the project, initiative, or company by keeping the passion for the cause in the forefront. They do the work by focusing behavior and effort on what needs to be done versus what they want. Leaders constantly ask, "What can I do to make a difference?" and are demanding of themselves and others in answering that question.

Readiness and Reflection

1. On a piece of paper or in your journal, describe a situation, issue, or cause you felt strongly about. Describe why this situation created such a passion and desire in you to act. Describe what you did to address this desire.

2. List the three most important professional desires you have. Describe what makes them so compelling for you. List what you will do in the next year to fulfill these professional passions.

3. On a scale of 1 to 3, with 1 being the lowest and 3 being the highest, rate your energy, enthusiasm, and determination to fulfill the professional passions listed in number 2 above. For the lowest scored item(s), talk with a mentor about strategies to improve it (them).

4. Describe whom you see in the mirror today. Describe whom you would like to see at the end of a year.

5. Describe how, in your professional life, you are committed to a purpose higher than yourself. How would you change this description?

6. Describe how you are making a difference in your daily professional life.

7. Reflect on what you have identified, through the reading and from the exercises, as your display of passion. Write a paragraph about where you are today as a passionate leader.

8. Develop two strategies for improving your passion, and add them to your personal leadership development plan.

"Leaders have an obligation to never let go of their passion and their commitment."

Part II

Being Set

One thing is certain about leaders: There would be none without followers. Leaders do not operate in a vacuum. No matter how compelling their purpose and values—how authentic, trustworthy, or passionate—they will not go far without people joining them. People follow leaders willingly if they believe the leader is honest, forward-looking, competent, and inspiring (Kouzes & Posner, 2007). Followers also value leaders who clearly articulate their passion and vision, intently listen to other points of view, and model ways and behaviors to reach the vision.

Leaders, on the other hand, seek followers who share common values, have the same high degree of commitment that the leaders have, and who possess complementary competencies for getting the job done. While followers look for the inspirational pull of vision, leaders look for the "right people on the bus in the right seats," while "getting the wrong people off" (Collins, p. 63, 2001). This notion of first deciding *who*, then later deciding *what*, has transformed lives, projects, businesses, and organizations.

Being set to lead others extends self-discovery to being an example, aligning actions as a leader to shared values with others.

Chapter 5

Gaze Into My Crystal Ball: Creating Shared Vision and Being Forward-Looking

Leaders delegate many tasks to those around them—finance monitoring, project management, trending, hiring, and even strategic planning or business planning. But effective leaders never relinquish their personal commitment to vision, which is what powers the enterprise. Simply put, a *vision* is an image of what can be; it is an expression of hopes, dreams, and aspiration for what the future ideally holds.

Visions are about achieving something significant, making a difference. They stretch us to think about the ideal and to draw meaning, purpose, and possibilities from what we do. The leader's job is to craft an embraceable vision for the team. A leader's vision is about doing something notable, larger than himself or herself. Leaders want to achieve what no one else has or can achieve, not because their aspirations are so different from other leaders but because their vision comes from an intrinsic, unique source—themselves.

> *"Leaders have to inspire themselves before they can inspire others."*

Before a leader can effectively guide others, a personal vision for the issue or situation has to be clear in the leader's mind. As Kouzes' and Posner's research (2007) validates, leaders have to believe in something themselves before they can ask others to believe. Leaders have to inspire themselves before they can inspire others. Other research has also found that external motivation is likely to create compliance or defiance, whereas self- or internal motivation often produces superior results (Bennis, 2003; Collins, 2001).

People who are self-motivated will keep working toward a goal even if there is no external, tangible reward. People who have reward or punishment as their external motivator stop their work once reward or punishment has been meted out (Kouzes & Posner, 2007). For leaders and their followers, internal motivation is optimal.

 ## Creating a Compelling Vision

I'm reminded of one summer when my son was working for a national clothing store. The company's vision statement, one that could potentially motivate employees, was proudly displayed in all stores. "Customers and Quality First" declared the signage. Unfortunately, the leader in the store where my son worked emphasized the sales objectives of the store, placing little emphasis on customers and quality. Additional bonus pay, attached to sales volume, was the external motivator.

The first week a sales quota was in force, my son failed to meet the target, despite his best efforts. After three weeks with no change, he came home discouraged and ready to quit. We encouraged him to tough it out and see if there was something he could do differently to increase his sales. He returned to work because he needed the money. By the sixth or seventh week, he was meeting and exceeding quotas. He would come home from work enthused, relating how well his shift had gone, and he was eager to return the next time. Curious, I asked him about the change.

One day while on break, he told me, he saw the vision statement, really read it, and changed his approach. Instead of hawking the latest promotional item, he tried to understand what his customers were looking for and helped them find the clothing that would suit their needs and purposes. He pointed out how well the item was made and what guarantees, conveniences, and instructions went with it. He was paying attention and found significance in the vision statement "Customers and Quality First." As a result, his sales and take-home pay soared.

Given the fact that self-inspired, motivated people are needed for success, effective leaders assume responsibility for creating and nurturing the conditions in which people work. The leader must give work and life a sense of meaning, purpose, and significance by offering an exhilarating vision. Getting to this exciting vision can take some time. It starts with the leader's self-discovery, but two other elements are clearly needed:

1. The vision should be so compelling that people relate and are motivated to share in it.

2. It is forward-looking, yet balanced with reality.

Shared Vision

Imagine you are a mid-level manager in an organization with the following vision:

> Be an integrated, values-driven health care system that promotes and advances a healthy community by focusing on the patient and partnering with health care professionals.

This institution's vision has been built around the needs of the patient, with the belief that healthy people create healthy communities. The vision is further focused by the acknowledgment that values, caring for the whole patient, and partnering with diverse health care professionals are important to the organization's future.

The fact that you accepted a position in this institution suggests you hold the same beliefs and values—that the vision is in alignment with your purpose. Although you did not personally create the vision, you share it and have chosen to be a key player in bringing it to reality. When this is true for all members of the team, the phenomenon of shared vision in the workplace occurs.

The role of the leader is to nurture and develop an environment that is shared-vision friendly, whether the vision originates with the leader or emanates from the organization, institution, or project. In creating such an environment and culture, the leader becomes a messenger and teacher of the vision. At the same time, he or she must enlist others and help them see how their individual dreams, interests, and hopes are aligned with those of the organization, project, or team. By helping team members see this alignment, leaders and their followers commit to a shared dream and are mobilized.

To reach a shared vision, leaders have to be clear about their own vision for the work ahead. Then, they must set to work on understanding, building, and confirming the values of individual team members. By talking to team members about their values and how they align with the values of the organization or project, leaders enable followers to move from being externally motivated contributors to being internally motivated. Once team values have been aligned, the leader then guides the followers in identifying and aligning their actions with those values.

For example, the team that values timeliness and efficiency will identify getting to meetings on time, having assignments done when promised, and seeking assistance from external experts when necessary as key actions and behaviors for their team. Team members—with their leader's direction—establish their ways of work. Through these actions, they set an example for each other. Only by sharing values and aligning them with action can leaders develop a shared vision.

Leaders create shared-vision teams in many ways, but the most important is listening to individual team members and engaging them, both individually and collectively, in dialogue. Through sharing and interaction, leaders and followers discover common purpose (Matusak, 1997).

Effective leaders find it useful to work with their team to identify a theme, one that gives expression to collective passion and draws on past learning and experiences. In creating a shared vision, leaders will imagine future possibilities, yet be grounded in reality and willing to test ideas. Once the vision is established, the leader keeps it front and center, repeatedly visualizing and affirming it (Kouzes & Posner, 2007). When these elements are practiced, work is cohesive and purpose-focused.

Collective Vision

Fifteen years ago, Sam was a senior leader for an education resource development company that developed preparation products for professional credentialing for individuals, schools, and businesses. The company's clients spanned the professional gamut from attorneys to accountants to health care professionals. A new credentialing process was emerging in the technology field. Sam was given the assignment of developing a preparatory resource for the process.

While not a "techie," Sam knew that he would have to appeal to the technology world to attract members of the potential client base to his company's product. He imagined a preparatory course offered through academic institutions via an electronic platform in which individuals worked through sophisticated technology issues. At his first team meeting, he shared his vision. He then asked each team member what his or her vision of the final product was. He listened intently, challenged their fears, talked and listened some more, exposed them to technology experts to increase their learning and understanding, and gave them new experiences in using technology in a learning environment. Collectively, the team developed a shared sense of purpose over time that became even larger than Sam's original one.

Before widespread use of computers and the Internet, Sam and his team envisioned and developed a computer-based platform for course instruction. Not only did they accomplish Sam's original vision, they also articulated his vision into a much larger one that had tremendous influence on their organization. In collaborating with his team to create the vision and build a plan to achieve that vision, Sam exercised and used skills to think and dream big, to engage all who were involved, and to allow himself to both lead and follow.

A truly effective leader, one who nurtures a shared-vision work environment, will have a team that clearly understands and acts on the vision and is able to articulate to others how its work contributes to the vision.

Forward-Looking, Reality-Based Visions

Visions are pictures of the future. A shared vision is nothing but rhetoric if it is not based on reality. Quinn (2004) terms this "grounded vision" and provides a crystal-clear definition:

> Grounded vision: Factual while hopeful and looking forward. This person conceptualizes and communicates a future that emerges from realities of the existing situation while integrating the possibilities of the future. The integration of reality and possibilities creates an image that attracts self and others to go outside their comfort zone and into a state of active creation. (Quinn, 2004, p. 140)

Being forward-looking while communicating a grounded vision is a distinguishing characteristic of effective leaders. This means leaders need to think, read, and talk about what lies ahead for their teams and organizations. Studying the future helps a leader create a vision and plan action and movement based on trends, facts, and lived experiences. Forward-looking leaders consider potential developments and effect change in the desired direction.

Leaders as futurists emphasize the macro versus the micro. They are people-orientated versus egocentric, and they are open-minded possibility thinkers rather than status quo doers. Futuristic leaders look inside out, basing their vision and action not just on trends and facts, but also on what is valued and learned from lived experience.

"Visions are pictures of the future. A shared vision is nothing but rhetoric if it is not based on reality."

Leaders use many tools to consider the future and how to influence it. They actively scan and monitor the environment in which they function. They map trends and plot shifts. They consider logical consequences of their actions, not just immediate impact, but impact on future generations as well. As a result of their study, futuristic leaders also create stories and scenarios about natural or expected events, and they actively engage in conversation about their discoveries and course of action. In sum, leaders who are forward-looking consider what could happen, what indicators point to this happening, and what needs to occur to precipitate this future happening.

Making the Future Happen

Several years ago, a family member was hospitalized for major surgery. After the surgeon skillfully repaired the damage, we were left in the capable hands of two nurses for three days of recovery. Every day, these nurses engaged in forward-looking, reality-thinking, fact-based care. Their vision was to successfully transition my loved one from post-surgery to home without complications and with full functional ability. Here is how they did it.

Knowing (fact) that pneumonia, infection, clots, and skin breakdown were possible complications (trends) of this surgery and wanting a complication-free recovery (future), they turned the patient regularly, placed a sheepskin under him, had him wear compression hosiery, frequently checked circulation, and supervised regular breathing and coughing exercises.

Knowing (fact) that the more effectively post-surgical pain is managed the quicker the recovery (trend), the nurses sought to make the patient as pain-free as possible to avoid prolonging recovery and further complications (future). They regularly assessed pain levels, periodically repositioned the patient to improve comfort, and administered analgesics prior to treatments and therapies that created discomfort.

Knowing (fact) that immobility weakens muscles and the ability of the patient to recover (trend), the nurses promoted flexibility by encouraging movement that would enhance recovery (future). They passively exercised all extremities, got the patient up and moving as soon as permitted, and helped the patient with exercises to strengthen upper extremities that would be used more than usual in the rehabilitation phase.

Of course, there were many more actions these nurses did, such as helping the patient maintain a positive frame of mind through humor and conversation, which is proven to speed recovery. They also provided a nutritious diet that the patient liked, as appropriate nutrition speeds healing.

Looking ahead to what could happen and was desired—a recovery without complication—the nurses based their actions on knowledge and reality. These caregivers were no different than many of us—no big titles or ego, no big companies—simply ordinary people with the vision to help people get well and back to their lives, proving once again that leaders come in all shapes and sizes. As Bennis and Nanus say: "Only a few will lead nations, more will lead companies. But legions will lead departments, communities, and small groups of people" (Bennis & Nanus, 2007).

Readiness and Reflection

1. After reading the statements, consider how they best describe or apply to you. Use 1 for *regularly*, 2 for *seldom*, or 3 for *not at all*.

   _____ I am aware of what is going on in the work environment around me.

   _____ I am clear about my role in this environment.

   _____ I take time to examine and think about trends in my industry.

   _____ I am content with how I see myself contributing to my work environment.

   _____ I believe I am living up to my full potential.

   _____ Others are pleased to be working with me.

   _____ I am clear about what needs to be accomplished in the future.

   _____ The team I work with has identified common ground and shared vision.

   _____ I remind people with whom I work of our shared vision by relating action to vision.

   _____ I talk with team members about their individual values and our team values.

   _____ I imagine future possibilities for my team and me.

   _____ I use macro- not micro-thinking.

   _____ I am open-minded.

   _____ I work for and serve a good greater than myself.

2. Reflect on your responses and write a paragraph about where you are today in your ability to create a shared vision that is forward-looking and reality-based.

3. Select four or five of your *seldom* or *not at all* responses that you would like to improve on. Develop two or three concrete actions you can take to improve these areas of visioning and futures thinking.

4. Hold a meeting with your team or co-workers where the only agenda item is your collective shared vision and what each will do to achieve it.

5. Read a biography of a leader you admire. Note the strategies, characteristics, behaviors, and values they demonstrate. What do you admire most about this person? What did he or she do that you would like to emulate?

6. Reflect on what you have learned from this chapter and these exercises. Write a paragraph about where you see yourself today in these competency areas.

7. Develop two strategies to improve your ability to create a shared vision and add them to your personal leadership development plan.

Chapter 6

Come, Follow Me: Inspiring and Motivating Others

Leaders are the ultimate cheerleaders of the world. Their job is to be fully self-aware and create the vision, but they must also inspire and motivate people to follow them. Leaders have to keep people moving in the right direction despite obstacles. They must appeal to the basic but often untapped need, value, and desire of others to contribute and make a difference. Leaders must know their followers and speak their language. They take the time to learn about their constituents' dreams, hopes, and needs, and they act in the best interests of those constituents.

Enthusiastic, energetic, and positive leaders help those around them see possibilities. They forge unity of purpose and show followers how their work contributes to the organization's vision and the greater good. Leaders have the ability to ignite passion through vivid language and expressive style and provide followers the opportunity and environment to live out their own aspirations. Leaders live life with animation and, in championing the vision, cheer others on to become champions.

> *"Leaders must know their followers and speak their language."*

Inspiring Others

To inspire literally means to infuse, breathe life into, or stimulate (Webster, 2004). For leaders, being an inspiration encompasses the ability to infuse life into vision by creating an environment that stimulates creative thought and action, prompting those in the environment to be energized by it. Leaders accomplish things because they inspire those around them to give their hearts and their best to the cause.

All of us want to be part of something bigger than ourselves, and all of us want to be valued and appreciated. Leaders create a culture where followers are not inspired by threats, cajoling, fear, or even pay, but by purpose, passion, and trust. How they do this is as diverse as the leaders themselves but, to be inspirational for others, five factors generally come into play at some point in the journey (Baldoni, 2005).

1. *Leaders who inspire share their passion with such enthusiasm that it becomes infectious.* Leaders who inspire communicate this passion and mission often, to everyone, and they help others connect the dots between what they do and how it fulfills the mission. They give meaning to the work.

   For example, the mail clerk in a large-membership organization may regard his or her job as mundane, not really addressing the professional development needs of the members (the mission). The inspirational leader will point out to that person that, among all the available choices, members have opted to be affiliated with their organization. The organization brings value to them, and being a card-carrying member is important. The promptness and efficiency with which the mail clerk gets cards mailed out is, therefore, also very important to the organization and its mission. By promptly sending out cards that entitle members to the services of the organization, the mail clerk contributes to the members' professional development.

2. *Leaders who inspire listen to and engage others in defining the shared meaning, goals, and action plan of the work.* Being inclusive and involving others connect work action to vision. To achieve a goal, it needs to be defined. We need clarity about what is expected of us. Inspirational leaders provide this definition and clarity, and take it a step further by making sure that people who follow their leadership understand the importance of their role in achieving the goal.

   For example, Larry, a mid-level manager, brought his in-service education team together to develop an electronic newsletter to improve information flow for members of the department's nursing staff. Lack of communication was causing people to miss out on programs they wanted to participate in. Larry presented his idea for a newsletter, describing how he envisioned it would look and what it might contain, but instead of formulating the entire solution on his own, he asked for input from the team. As a result, team members recognized what they could contribute to the project: One was a good writer; one had good information networks, another had design skills, and still another possessed technology skills. Together, they formulated a plan of action for publishing the newsletter, and they delivered the first issue within six weeks of their initial discussion.

3. *Leaders who inspire set the pace and are front-line participants.* Inspirational leaders ennoble the cause and the work by their willingness to "get their hands dirty."

As the director of nursing for an extended-care facility, Dana never failed to show up on Friday mornings to spend time on the units, giving baths or medications. This simple act spoke volumes to her employees, conveying that she would never ask them to do something she would not do. Employees respected her passion and commitment for the patients and for them. By setting the pace and showing that she was part of the team, just as the front-line nurses and assistants were, and that she felt enough pride in their work to join them, Dana was letting her employees know how meaningful their work was.

> *"Inspirational leaders trust the people around them to do the work of the organization or company."*

4. *Leaders who inspire help people believe in themselves.* Many leaders do this by looking for opportunities to "catch" people doing things right and making a point of mentioning this to the employee. Inspirational leaders trust the people around them to do the work of the organization or company. They emphasize the personal power of those people to make a difference in fulfilling the vision. We all have a choice whether or not to commit to the organization's aspirations through our work, but making the decision to support

the organization's goals is much easier when the leader trusts and respects our efforts.

Consider Cindy, whom many referred to as the walk-around boss. At the beginning of her shift, Cindy would visit briefly with each of her team members. During these sessions, she would always find a way to comment on each person's contribution toward the health goals of the patients they were caring for. The staff looked forward to these daily desk or bedside chats and felt energized by her feedback. As a result of Cindy's interest in her team members and their patients, her team had fewer errors and higher patient satisfaction levels than any other team. Her continual reinforcement of the vision and team members' contributions to its fulfillment inspired them to believe in their abilities to get the job done.

5. *Leaders who inspire appreciate value and enjoy the work of leading others.* They are free with praise when it is deserved and help people work through their weaknesses. They readily admit their own errors or need for help and are often self-deprecating and open about their own mistakes. They provide opportunities for other people and themselves to grow and develop, thus promoting an environment of learning. Inspirational leaders celebrate successes, big and small, and have fun. This attitude conveys to those around them that, while working for a greater good is serious, it can also be enjoyable.

Betty, a senior-level marketing person in a well-known communication firm, was faced with a personnel situation when Janet, a top senior manager, made a serious error in communicating with a client. Betty, seeing this as an opportunity to help Janet learn from her mistake, called Janet to her office to review the situation and to collaborate with her on a solution.

During their conversation, Janet was hostile toward the client and quite defensive in her responses to Betty. By telling Janet about some of her own mistakes in dealing with difficult clients, Betty was able to help Janet see that allowing personal opinions to interfere with professional action was not in the best interest of the company's mission. She also helped Janet realize that her obligation was to serve the client, and the need at that moment was to clear up the communication error. Rather than sending Janet off to take care of the problem alone, Betty helped her craft a response to the client's concerns and outline remedial actions she would take to correct the error. She invested in and valued Janet helping her discover ways to maximize her work.

In summary, leaders who inspire make people feel they are at the heart of things. They connect with the people they are working with, whether in an organization or a community. At a deep level, they share themselves, their emotions, and experiences, and create hospitable space for those around them to do the same.

Motivating Others

Motivation is an inner drive or intention that compels a person to act. Mage (2008) calls it the intersection of reason and emotion, because motivation is derived from motive—the reason why—and from emotion, the energy that gets us into motion. To compel action on the part of followers, leaders have to create an environment that supports and encourages the person's inner drive, making sure it is aligned with the organization's vision. Leaders cannot inspire people if they don't know what is important to their followers. Likewise, leaders cannot motivate others unless they know what is meaningful to themselves, their followers, and the organization.

People are motivated when they perceive that benefits outweigh negative consequences, and they make decisions accordingly. While fear motivates, it has a short life span because the source is not internal to the person. People choose what enhances their own sense of worth and what fulfills their desire to be accepted, competent, contributory, and recognized. In addition, they choose what allows them to have control over their lives. Use of fear and cajoling does not provide the self-satisfaction or autonomy that people need to sustain their energy and emotion. It is the leader's job to see that these basic human needs are met. Leaders, realizing that motivating is an ongoing process and not an occasional task, establish a supportive environment that fuels people's motivation. They give attention to the climate and tone of the environment and keep people moving in the right direction by finding out and speaking to what is of significance to those they are leading. Leaders consistently do five things to tap into people's motivation (Clark, 2008).

1. *Leaders who motivate first gain an understanding of what* they *find motivating, and then seek to understand what motivates their followers.* Have you ever noticed in your work or community life that what the leader experiences is often what the followers experience? If the leader is stressed, so are their followers. If they are isolated and perform work in isolation, so do their followers. If they are energetic and energized, so are their followers. People look to leaders to establish the tone for the environment in which they function. It is important, therefore, for leaders to identify what motivates them and align that with what motivates their followers. If the leader is motivated by money and results at any cost, so are his or her followers, but if the leader is motivated to do good work and make a difference in his or her job, followers will be similarly motivated.

   What motivates people is as different as they are, so leaders tap into motivators that are of the most significance to the individual. By discovering what those individual motivators are, the leader gives followers a sense of value and respect for who they are, what they do, and what has meaning for them. One-on-one conversations in which leaders ask, listen, and learn from their followers are one of the most effective ways leaders create a motivational environment.

2. *Leaders who motivate articulate the vision of the organization, company, or team in a way that resonates for their audience.* The leader stresses benefits and conveys how the actions of the followers contribute to the team or company. The leader thereby gives a sense of achievement to the person or group, letting them know they are working toward a greater purpose.

"Pointing out how the person makes the vision happen is a powerful motivator."

In talking with a group of administrative assistants, the leader might emphasize that accurate data and information gathering is important, as it enables the team or leader to make decisions about future directions of the team or company. Or a leader might emphasize to the customer service staff that answering client calls and questions in a timely manner, pleasant tone, and with reliable information is a major contributor to keeping a loyal customer base. Pointing out how the person makes the vision happen is a powerful motivator.

3. *Leaders who motivate involve those around them in work-related decisions.* To do this, leaders readily delegate and expect staff members to unleash their talents and skills on the tasks or issues at hand. Effective leaders challenge people to reach attainable goals and recognize that the gifts of others enable the achievement of those goals. This gives people a sense of control over their own destiny and a sense of autonomy. An effective project leader will turn over certain aspects of a project to the person best equipped to handle them and step back—providing guidance and counsel when needed—while that team member puts his or her talents to use.

4. *Leaders who motivate serve as a coach and role model providing feedback.* What leaders do speaks much louder than what they say, so demonstrating genuine interest in followers and investing time in them are good investments of the leader's time and are effective in motivating people to work for the good of the team, project, or company. This attention and concern give a sense of support and enhance self-esteem.

> *"In its purest design, motivation is the primary form of self-inspiration, and leaders create an environment for its expression."*

The leader who regularly discusses performance, offers suggestions for improvement, and provides opportunity to develop needed skills reaps far more benefits than the leader who discusses these items once a year; but feedback, coaching, and relationships alone won't create an environment that motivates. The leader has to live out his or her own motivation and provide systems that support what motivates others.

The system may be as simple as a team deciding how decisions are made and the ways they will work together, or as complex as an organization's policy and procedures for compensating and evaluating performance. Whatever the form, supports must be in place to enhance the leader's ability to create an energized, motivating environment.

5. *Leaders who motivate recognize and reward the work of motivated people.* We all want to know our efforts are appreciated and are moving our group toward its goals and vision. By recognizing, celebrating, and rewarding, leaders give a sense of accomplishment, boost the desire to contribute more, and feed the intrinsic need of people to be good at what they do.

 Internalizing Motivation

Melani was a patient care coordinator on a maternity unit in a large, urban women's health hospital. She supervised 20 nurses and 20 assistants. She was also a well-respected member of the interdisciplinary team of physicians, respiratory therapists, and nutritionists who planned care for mothers—often high-risk—on the unit.

She had a vision that all mothers, regardless of their delivery type and anesthesia, should have an opportunity to be with their newborns immediately after birth. The practice of the unit was for anesthetized mothers to be separated from their babies until the mother was up and walking. This often meant a delay in breast-feeding and mothers bonding with their infants. To be successful, Melani knew she needed a well-crafted project plan, administrative support, and team buy-in for her vision. She knew her biggest challenge was to get people to change from their status quo practices.

Melani ceaselessly talked about the benefits of maternal-infant bonding. She pointed out how little the new practice would disrupt routines. She provided reading materials and held in-service training. She brought in treats and pizza. She garnered support, but she irritated some people. After a few months of working to shift the practice, she knew something more was needed to motivate staff members to support her vision. The homemade goodies and pizza lunches had not done the trick!

In talking with people, Melani noted that the largest objection to changing current practice was mothers coming to the nursery during peak hours. The staff just could not handle one more task during those times. However, unit staff members were more than willing to transport newborns once mothers were awake. By adopting this practice—an external motivator that didn't add to the work of the nursery staff—Melani was able to motivate them to accept change. It got her foot in the door.

Then, an interesting thing began to happen. Initially, the practice was that the floor nurse would call the nursery to let them know they were coming to get the newborn of the mom who had awakened. But before they could walk down the hall to get the baby, the nursery staff was already bringing the baby to the mom. This went unacknowledged a few times, mostly because Melani was not around to see it.

One day she was there and, naturally, asked why the nursery person was bringing the baby to the mom. Staff members responded that they got a great deal of satisfaction from seeing the mom's first look at her baby and didn't want to miss out on this joy. The motivation had become internal.

While people are responsible for their own happiness and what intrinsically motivates them, leaders have the ability to uncover and unleash factors that stimulate this motivation. In its purest design, motivation is the primary form of self-inspiration, and leaders create an environment for its expression.

Readiness and Reflection

1. Check all the statements that apply to you. As a leader:

    _____ I clearly state what I expect of my group.

    _____ I act in a way that reflects commitment to the group.

    _____ I convey concern for those I work with.

    _____ I make every effort to keep those I work with up to date.

    _____ I give those in my group the opportunity to express their expectations.

    _____ I understand what my primary inspiration and motivation are.

    _____ I make people feel as if they belong.

    _____ I delegate readily.

    _____ I clearly communicate to each person their value and contribution to our work.

    _____ I ask, listen, and learn from others.

    _____ I actively engage others in goal setting and action planning.

    _____ I provide opportunities for others to lead.

    _____ I have fun at work.

    _____ I see others having fun.

2. Based on your responses, write a paragraph on where you see yourself as an inspirational and motivating leader today. Write a second paragraph describing what you will do to create a more inspiring and motivating environment for your team.

3. Make a list of the people you lead or interact with—team members, vendors, customers, and colleagues—and identify what you believe motivates them. Draft the same list for yourself. Review both lists and identify common motivators. Plan an activity that addresses one of these motivators. For example, a common motivator may be recognition for a job well done, and you can consider spotlighting, weekly, one of the team members.

4. Return to the biography of the visionary leader that you read in fulfilling the Readiness and Reflection assignments of Chapter 5, and make a list of factors or events that motivated this person. Make a list of the ways in which he or she inspired others.

5. List five things you can do in the next week that will provide opportunity for others to feel inspired or motivated.

6. E-mail three colleagues and ask them to share where their inspiration comes from and what motivates them most.

7. Reflect on what you have learned about motivating and inspiring others. Write a paragraph about where you are today in demonstrating this competency.

8. Develop two strategies to improve your skills in motivating and inspiring others, and add them to your personal leadership development plan.

Chapter 7

Do We Speak The Same Language?
Communicating and Listening

"To be meaningful, communication has to be regarded as true and relevant for those engaged in it."

Leaders may have an abundance of values, vision, and passion, but if they are not able to communicate and listen effectively, those assets can yield little. Communication, like leadership, is relational and transactional. It is a process centered on continual, evolving exchanges between people in order to reach a shared meaning.

Being a good communicator is a succeed-or-fail issue for a leader. Effective communication gives life to the vision, interaction, and work that is being pursued. When communication is poor, uncertainty and chaos may ensue, creating an environment where vision, meaning, and understanding cannot thrive.

Leaders recognize the importance of communication and listening, knowing that their total effectiveness rises and falls in direct proportion to their ability to communicate meaningfully (Matusak, 1997, DeVito, 2007). Good leaders pay attention to the modes of communication—verbal, nonverbal, and behavioral—as well as to the context in which it occurs—situational, organizational, and cultural. They continually develop their communication skills knowing the effect that excellent communication and listening can have on their relationships, credibility, and integrity.

Communication

"In its simplest definition, communication is the exchange of information, thoughts, and messages between two or more people."

We all believe we are effective communicators—it's just that people around us don't understand our message! In its simplest definition, communication is the exchange of information, thoughts, and messages between two or more people. People, who bring their own experiences, expectations, and intentions to bear on the exchange add an extra dynamic to this definition. It is no wonder, then, that developing the art of communication can be difficult, especially when the real purpose of communication—shared meaning and understanding—is factored in. Leaders accept and master this challenge by being pacesetters, strategists, listeners, and doers.

Communication Pacesetter

Leaders who practice the art of communication set the tone and pace of how information and messages are conveyed. They astutely craft and deliver their communications by tailoring them to the target audience. They also assess how the message or information is received, adapting accordingly.

Leaders recognize that language patterns influence people's abilities to receive and understand the message. We all know people who leave out essential information in a communication, requiring the receiver to fill in the blanks. Other communications are distorted by the way the sender perceives and experiences the world. Personal prejudices shift the tone, wording, and climate of the communication. Barriers and gaps are created in communications when people use jargon or acronyms; mumble or speak too quickly (speed speak); or use menacing, questioning, whining, or angry tones of voice. Nonverbal cues such as facial expression, eye contact, or posture affect the sending and receiving of communication as well as physical barriers such as desks. For example, the person who sits forward behind a desk or table with their arms tightly crossed over their chest conveys a closed reception to the communication whereas the person who sits back in the chair with arms draped over their lap while facing the

chair of the other person actually communicates more openness.
Since communication is a two-way process, the sender is responsible for
conveying messages precisely while the receiver is responsible for
clarifying what was said, if shared meaning and understanding are to be
accomplished.

 ## Be Open, Inviting, and Clarifying

Joseph is the team leader for five people who are charged with
launching a new product. He calls his team together and begins
communicating with the team by validating the need for the
product, its relationship to the company mission, the need for the
contributions of each team member and opening the conversation
up by saying:

"We have been assigned the task of launching this new educational
product in six months. Our market research shows high interest and
demand for it, and providing this resource certainly fulfills our
mission to be innovators and leaders in this area. Each of you bring
an expertise in some aspect of this products launch, and we all need
your best individual effort to meet our timeframe. I am confident we
can meet our objectives and make a significant difference for the
company and our clients, but I need your input before we start to
review the timeline and actions I previously sent you."

This communication style is open, inviting, and clarifying as Joe
establishes shared significance for the work of the team.

To be meaningful, communication has to be regarded as true and
relevant for those engaged in it. Only through mutual understanding is
rapport established between sender and receiver. An essential component
of communication rapport is achieved when people trust each other and
experience alignment of behaviors, words, and responses. The greater the
rapport, the greater the trust, which in turn reinforces common ground
between sender and receiver.

Rapport occurs when body language, verbal language, and tone between receiver and server match in a positive way. I had a boss early in my career who had good intentions but poor communication skills. During meetings, he always appeared to be flustered and in a hurry. He would multitask—looking for folders, checking his calendar, or signing documents—throughout the discussions. He interrupted frequently to offer his solutions to the issue under discussion, spoke so quickly that most of what he said was lost, and continually used jargon that none of us understood.

"Keeping stakeholders well-informed requires that leaders have the ability to analyze, summarize, synthesize, paraphrase, express feeling, disclose personal information, admit mistakes and errors, solicit divergent views, respond nondefensively, and ask for clarification.

Oftentimes staff would leave a meeting more confused than before. His behaviors and the environment he created did not facilitate shared understanding and meaning on critical issues, including such primary concerns as patient-care protocols. Consequently, our rapport and productivity suffered.

Leaders who are good communicators have a communication plan and goals in place for themselves and for their team or organization. They establish a culture and climate of open, positive communication, sometimes by using guidelines, but, mostly through action and behavior. The importance of culture cannot be overstated in terms of its effect on communications, and the leader is the one who has to set the pace for what the culture should be.

Culture is a pattern of assumptions and actions that have become integrated into the way people work and relate with one another. It is the way things get done, or the "rules of the game." The culture dictates how people communicate. Effective leaders demonstrate and expect free flow of information, thoughts, and ideas.

There are, of course, circumstances when confidentiality is appropriate in communications. In general, however, effective leaders should share everything possible to keep co-workers and colleagues so well-supplied with correct information they have what they need to get their jobs done. Keeping stakeholders well-informed requires that leaders have the ability to analyze, summarize, synthesize, paraphrase, express feeling, disclose personal information, admit mistakes and errors, solicit divergent views, respond nondefensively, and ask for clarification. Behaviors such as these build a positive communication culture.

"The importance of culture cannot be overstated in terms of its effect on communications, and the leader is the one who has to set the pace for what the culture should be."

 ## How Culture Can Affect Communication

An example of culture affecting communication is illustrated by a story from a nurse friend who took a senior-level position in a large not-for-profit organization, only to realize two weeks into the job that staff members brought everything to her for a decision or just to share. While she was glad to have this information, she quickly realized she was the only person they were sharing it with. They were not telling colleagues who had the talents and skills to help them—only her, the boss. Stepping back to look at established communication patterns, she discovered that most departments worked in "silos," that one department did not know what the other was doing, and information was hoarded rather than shared.

This lack of sharing had been established by the previous boss, who wanted to control information flow on an as-needed basis. Unfortunately, this caused bottlenecks that reduced efficiency and productivity, because people did not have the information needed to get their jobs done, either solely or in cooperation with others. It became quite obvious to my friend that this communication culture would not work for her vision and leadership style of community-building and collaboration.

Communication Strategist

To effectively implement communication strategies, leaders have to understand the styles and needs of those they are working with. They also have to practice what they wish to see in those around them. Understanding involves listening, and practice involves behavior.

Followers look to their leaders to be positive and open-minded, and to use powerful, energetic language. They respond to leaders who place their whole being into how they communicate, regardless of the modality of communication. Leaders practice what they preach by setting up an infrastructure that promotes the type of communication they believe will best achieve desired results for their team and organization.

My friend who walked into a culture of closed-communication silos began having open planning meetings. Instead of a small group of senior staff meeting behind closed doors, she opened up strategy planning to the entire staff. At monthly meetings, employees actively engaged in developing and choosing alternatives and became part of the decision-making process.

People did not open up until they realized she was serious about their engagement in the process and their investment of talent and time. To foster the new culture, she included measures as part of annual employee appraisals. As people recognized the stake they had in the process—not only for themselves but also to make a difference for the organization—trust, compassion, collaboration, and results changed direction.

Active Listener

Have you ever been in a conversation with someone and you noticed they were looking at someone else, answering instant messages, yawning, or having sidebar conversations? This has probably happened to all of us, but it seldom happens with a leader who is a good communicator.

Listening to or comprehending a message is not the same as hearing. Active listening is a multistep process the leader learns and masters. In communication, a message is received from the speaker. That seems simple enough, but the tendency is to shift our thinking to the response. Receiving requires focused attention—being fully present for the speaker.

Once the message is received, we try to learn the meaning of the message, both verbal and nonverbal. The leader analyzes content, context, and the speaker's perspective, asking questions and rephrasing what he has heard for clarity. The leader will also look for hidden meaning or deeper messages, those things that are often unspoken but discernable in tone, attitude, inference, or body language. Good listeners then use this analysis to help remember what was *actually* said, instead what they *think* was said.

They do this by focusing on the central idea presented. They evaluate the message and judge its motive and intent. Finally, the listener responds to both the central message and the deeper hidden ones (Devito, 2007). When listening, the leader conveys interest in what the speaker is saying by maintaining good eye contact, nodding and leaning slightly forward, reinforcing that he or she is listening by paraphrasing or asking questions, and providing a distraction-free and friendly space for the conversation.

Active listening by a leader to a person or a group is beneficial for both the sender and the leader. For the sender, it conveys the message that what he or she has to say is of value and interest—that his or her ideas, message, or information will make a difference. It increases trust, rapport, and motivation in the sender. For the leader, listening provides information on how people are thinking and feeling. It also provides a venue for presentation of new ideas and perspectives from which the leader can learn.

Active Listening

Growth was beginning to occur in the organization, particularly in membership, and it became increasingly clear that a leader was needed to direct the initiatives and processes. I approached a member of the staff and urged her to take on this responsibility, because of the leadership skill and style I was seeing her exercise in her mid-level position. She was reluctant at first, saying she knew very little about member recruitment and retention. This was outside of her area, and she questioned whether it was wise to put her in charge of such an important initiative. She was passionate, however, about learning and challenging herself, and she accepted the position.

Within a year, she had a full three-phase plan for member recruitment and retention. She had implemented tracking systems for member receipt of benefits and had opened a member call center. She increased the recruitment rate by 25 percent and the retention rate by 15 percent. At a time when the industry was experiencing declining membership, our organization was actually growing. This employee breathed life, productivity, efficiency, and results into the organization, and she did this by listening.

She listened to what members and potential members were saying; she listened to what her colleagues were saying and sharing with her; and she listened to what those outside the organization were saying about recruitment and retention. She listened, took advice, lost arguments, and followed advice. She asked powerful questions and willingly understood others' perspectives. She knew leading this department was a reciprocal relationship with many individuals and that she could not do it alone. She listened and asked others to join her on the journey to improved outcomes for members.

Communication Doer

Leaders who are good communicators invest in their own communication development. They become adept at communicating their message across modalities—whether written or oral, or informal or formal presentations—and they recognize which messages are appropriate for the specific modality.

Despite the convenience of e-mail, instant messaging, and other forms of electronic communication, research has repeatedly demonstrated that the most effective communication occurs face to face (Barrett, 2005). This is because it allows immediate feedback, provides multiple auditory and visual cues, is a natural language, and can be personalized. Face-to-face communication allows messages to be adjusted, clarified, and reinforced instantly.

Leaders who are good communicators practice the five C's of communication:

1. Clarity

2. Completeness

3. Correctness

4. Currency

5. Congruence.

While these may seem self-evident, here is what leaders do to make the five C's come alive.

For *clarity*, leaders choose words familiar to the audience. They communicate in short, effective sentences that accurately reflect their thoughts. They tend to use action words and vivid images, conveying positive messages. They tell stories and use metaphors and other aids to illustrate their points. They are sincere, tactful, open, and appreciative of their audience.

Leaders give *complete, correct* messages. They research, analyze, and rehearse what they are going to say or write to be sure their meaning is understandable. They do not assume the receiver will fully understand the context and take time to be thorough in reaching a shared meaning. They use accurate and current information, facts, and figures.

Lastly, leaders who are effective communicators deliver messages that contain *currency* and *congruence* for their audience—messages that connect the dots. They align what they are saying with goals, vision, and objectives. Even when the message is bad, the leader is careful to relate how the event or circumstance affects the vision and well-being of the organization, is diligent in avoiding blame, and maintains integrity.

Feedback

Giving and receiving feedback are among the most difficult talents for a leader to master. While most of us view feedback in a negative way, it is actually an opportunity to achieve positive results and improve work and relationships. In the end, we can accept or reject the feedback, but it provides a chance to change and possibly renew our personal impact within the workplace.

Feedback is, in essence, telling the truth as you see it. It is a form of communication that helps people discover their true selves and validate and improve their talents. Planning and giving effective feedback are important competencies for a leader. We have all experienced haphazard and ill-designed feedback, but good leaders realize that competence in interpersonal communication and an ability to handle people well add to their effectiveness by strengthening relationships and trust. Feedback is best received when excessive stress and distraction are minimized. For this reason, leaders pay attention to the time and place that feedback is given, making sure there are no interruptions. Leaders put the receiver at ease by asking permission to share insights they have developed.

A leader is also specific in his or her feedback, providing examples and observations. They explain their reaction and perceptions clearly and include suggestions for change, offering support. Leaders also frequently rehearse what they are going to say and anticipate the receiver's response, helping the receiver clearly understand their interactions and behaviors.

 ## Giving Good Feedback

A colleague had been working with a mid-level manager who was having difficulty relating to her subordinates. This colleague had observed that this person was often abrupt and quite authoritarian in her approach in team meetings and work conversations. She often went back to her subordinates to make sure they had followed through on tasks, many times finding the tasks completed well in advance of the due date, but offering very little positive feedback.

My colleague set up an appointment with the manager. Before the meeting, this leader carefully noted her observations, practiced what she would say, and made a list of how she could help this person change her style. During the meeting, my colleague explained to the manager that she wanted to share some observations and asked if this was OK. Given permission, she described in detail the specifics of the behaviors she had observed and carefully provided examples of alternative approaches the manager might consider.

She also told the manager that she had great potential to develop as a leader if she wanted to work on these behaviors and her style of interaction. The manager was at first taken aback, not realizing her manner and style were perceived in this way, but then she asked for help in developing new tactics for managing her team.

Together my colleague and the manager established a plan. My colleague took the time to set up a positive environment for the conversation, one where the manager could easily receive the feedback. She also wove suggestions for improvement into her comments about the behaviors that needed to change. Finally, she offered support and help to the manager, demonstrating her interest in the manager's improvement.

In addition to giving feedback, leaders actively seek feedback from others, seeing it as an opportunity for self-improvement. In receiving feedback from others, leaders have the opportunity to do the hard work of self-discovery—accepting limitations, being responsible for mistakes, and recognizing deficiencies. These self-examinations can be painful, but leaders who take advantage of the opportunity that feedback provides will discover how they affect and influence people.

> *"Good leaders accept responsibility for their shortcomings and make a choice to change."*

Good leaders also critique feedback in terms of reality. When receiving feedback, for example, ask the following questions:

- Have I received this feedback from more than one person?

- Does the person providing the feedback know a great deal about the subject?

- Is the feedback really about me, or is there a deeper meaning?

- How important is this feedback to me?

- Is this feedback from someone who has good intentions and standards?

Finally, leaders take responsibility for being honest with themselves about their interpersonal relationships, interactions, behaviors, decisions, and communications. They engage in self-feedback, recognizing when they made errors or were ill-prepared, and are open and honest about themselves to others. Rather than looking outside themselves to find reasons for errors and deficiencies, they take ownership and consider ways to prevent recurrences. Good leaders accept responsibility for their shortcomings and make a choice to change.

Readiness and Reflection

1. For the following questions, answer yes (Y) or no (N). When communicating with others, I regularly:

_____ Show interest in what they are saying.

_____ Give full attention to the interaction.

_____ Put people at ease.

_____ Display a natural sincerity and empathy.

_____ Maintain eye contact.

_____ Avoid judgment.

_____ Respect others' perspectives.

_____ Am not defensive.

_____ Let others do most of the talking.

_____ Seek to understand what the speaker really means—the message behind the message.

_____ Ask deep, clarifying questions when I don't understand.

_____ Approach others with respect, dignity, and trust.

_____ Offer praise and reprimands as appropriate.

_____ Have a communication plan and goals for myself and others.

_____ Give complete, correct, and congruent messages.

_____ Give clear messages.

_____ Analyze, synthesize, and summarize communications I have with others.

_____ Understand nonverbal behaviors.

_____ Provide feedback and support for change.

_____ Control my emotions in communications.

_____ Create best solutions for communication problems.

_____ Admit mistakes.

_____ Assess my own communication effectiveness.

2. For the responses you answered "no" to, make a list of new behaviors or approaches you can learn that will enable you to change your responses to "yes."

3. Spend part of a team meeting playing the "Rumor Game." It is best to have no fewer than six and no more than 10 participants in addition to yourself. Ask half of the group to be listeners and the other half to be note takers and observers. All listeners, except for one, leave the room. Now, give that listener a piece of information about your work environment or situation that could be real. Ask him or her to convey this to a second listener, who is then invited back into the room. The second listener repeats the information to the third, and the third to the fourth, and so on, until the information has been transmitted to all listeners. The note takers observe these interactions, noting when correct or incorrect information is given. Finally, the leader of the game debriefs the group by asking for note-taker feedback and by leading a discussion about the need for the five C's in communication and the implications of miscommunication.

4. Reflect on a conversation you have had in the past with someone who gave you feedback on your behaviors and communications. What did this person do or say that impressed you the most? What did they do or say that did not impress you? Did you take or leave their advice and feedback? Why?

5. Together with your team, role-play different scenarios that depict open, positive communication; closed, silo communication; and confusing, incomplete communication. Engage in a discussion about how each of these communication styles will help or hinder their work.

6. Develop a communication plan with your team, defining what and how you will communicate, what communication modalities and behavior are acceptable, and what the consequences are if acceptable behaviors are not met.

7. Reflect on what you have learned about communication from this chapter and the exercises. Write a paragraph about where you are today in your communication and listening competency.

8. Develop two strategies to improve your communication and listening skills and add them to your personal leadership development plan.

Chapter 8

Do As I Say AND As I Do: Modeling and Mentoring

Leaders use themselves as models to demonstrate the values they espouse. They set the example for what they profess to believe, what they hope to achieve in the vision, and what they are committed to. Modeling is behavior that shows congruence and alignment with belief and purpose.

Models are people who are considered the standard of excellence—someone to be imitated and followed because of their worth. Everything they do reflects the larger purpose and shared meaning, and their actions clearly show their commitment, earning them respect, credibility, and trust.

When followers are deciding whom to follow, they carefully observe what the leader does. If observation tells them the leader acts with alignment, honesty, and integrity, followers will sign on. If observation shows self-serving actions, the leader will be obeyed but not followed. In its literal sense, modeling is setting an example that is observed and emulated by the follower.

> "Models show consistency of deeds and words, but a mentor also willingly gives time, expertise, and emotion to a relationship."

Mentors are models, but they are also guides, teachers, guardians, and sages who actively invest in and interact with others to promote learning and development. Models show consistency of deeds and words, but a mentor also willingly gives time, expertise, and emotion to a relationship. Leaders are mentors as well as models. They walk the talk and invest in others relationally.

Role Models

The term *role model* was introduced and developed by Robert K. Merton, a world-renowned sociologist. Merton hypothesized that individuals compare themselves with reference groups of people who occupy a role to which the individual aspires. The term has passed into general usage to simply mean an individual who serves as an example of positive behavior and excellence.

In referring to people comparing themselves to a reference group, Merton noted that individuals were drawn to people with similar beliefs and values, but who were more experienced than themselves. These individuals both observe and imitate the behavior of the role model, frequently unbeknownst to the model. Examples of role modeling are all around us: preteens who want to look and act like the latest teen idol; high school athletes who connect with a sports coach and want to become pro athletes; young adults in their first jobs who have gregarious, successful bosses and want to be just like them; or people in mid-career who have leaders in their profession they admire and wish to emulate. Role models are all around us. *Good* role models are harder to find. Good role models live by their words and put others above themselves, making a commitment to do the right thing.

> *"In some ways, leadership is a performing art in which every action, word, and behavior is seen, critiqued, and processed by followers."*

The truest test of authentic and credible leadership is in what a leader pays attention to and what he or she does: In other words, the example a leader sets (Kouzes & Posner, 2007). In some ways, leadership is a performing art in which every action, word, and behavior is seen, critiqued, and processed by followers. Great leaders understand this, continually manage it, and pay attention to developing behavioral patterns that reinforce it.

Leaders give attention to how they spend their time. They devote agenda discussion time to values and vision; they interact with people they serve and work with; they ask questions and tell stories about how the vision is being realized; they establish an infrastructure that supports work standards and ethics; they create processes that encourage collaboration, openness, and a sense of contribution; and they make others feel they are appreciated and that their overall needs are being met.

In setting the example, leaders continually monitor and adapt how they respond. They put on the leader face everyday when they go to work, controlling the facial expressions of frustration, boredom, and disgust. Rather than exploding in anger, rolling their eyes, yawning, or sneering, they maintain an even-tempered appearance and demeanor. People look to the leader to be in control. Not only is "going off the deep end" unacceptable behavior, it is bad modeling.

Leaders also have the ability to edit as they speak and write. They place themselves in the position of the message receiver, focusing on the vocabulary, subject, and tone of the message and adjusting it for the audience's potential response. In addition, leaders role-model the ability to view their own behavior, not only through feedback but also by observing how others react.

Leaders who set the example take the high road and let people save face. They refuse to be engaged in manipulation, retaliatory behavior, or badmouthing. They give people the benefit of the doubt and get all the facts before passing judgment. And in meting out judgment, they are fair, composed, and act with class, striving to not demean others.

Setting an Example

Leaders who set the example are always looking for ways to reinforce their values and vision with actions. A great example of this comes from the autobiography of U.S. Army General Norman Schwarzkopf, who tells the story of taking command of a new division. He was running one day when he encountered a group of soldiers who ran past him like Olympians. Some distance behind them were half a dozen soldiers who had not been able to keep pace.

When the first group stopped, Schwarzkopf caught up with them, and the company commander proudly related that they had just completed their five-mile run. The general replied with words of praise and asked who the people in the back were. The company commander said they were the ones who couldn't keep up.

Schwarzkopf's response was one that reinforced his values of inclusion and sticking together. He asked the commander to imagine himself as a new recruit who had just come to his new unit, right out of basic training, and was feeling great about being a soldier. The new recruit realizes his new unit does a lot more running than he is used to. The first day he is out with them, he runs and runs until his legs give out, but his unit keeps going and leaves him behind. Then Schwarzkopf asked the commander, what kind of unit cohesion does that build? He did not berate the commander in front of his men; he merely challenged him to consider how he could build his men to be there for one another. The commander understood what his general was telling him: the group must stay together, come to rely on one another, and help each other if they are to be successful in their endeavors. The next day, to develop cohesion, the commander reorganized the run so that the faster runners were partnered with the slower ones, teaching them how to improve their speed and efficiency. No one was left behind again.

Schwarzkopf, in his wisdom, knew the episode would be talked about around the base and emulated by other units. He had his "leader face" on even when he was out for a morning run, he paid attention to how he spent his time and took the opportunity to talk with subordinates and teach his values, and he monitored what he said to let the commander save face by helping him come up with a solution.

Mentoring

The core of mentoring is people and interaction, two very dynamic, fluid, and changeable components of a relationship. As defined by Vance and Olson (1998), mentoring is a "developmental, empowering, nurturing relationship that extends over time in which mutual sharing, learning, and growth occur in an atmosphere of respect, collegiality, and affirmation" (p. 5). In the mentoring relationship, the process of self-realization, creativity, ability-awakening, developing new competencies and moving toward achievement of vision and goals is set into motion.

The relationship has two key players: the mentor, who is usually an established leader and authority—an expert in a specific field who is willing to guide, give time, and commit to the relationship; and the mentee or protégé, who is a leader-in-learning—a motivated, self-directed person who wants to avail him- or herself of the experiences and expertise of a seasoned person.

What motivates people to be mentors or mentees is quite diverse. Perhaps it is career or professional advancement, succession planning, or learning a new set of management or organizational skills. What mentoring always encompasses is learning and growth for both mentor and mentee.

Mentoring relationships catalyze our transformation as individuals, generating and releasing new capabilities we sometimes did not know we had. These relationships are nurturing, empowering, and reciprocal, and they create learning alliances in which truth, trust, and abundance are achieved.

True leaders naturally take on this role of mentoring, because they have an inherent need to serve others, as well as to learn and better themselves. They actively seek opportunities to share their passions and experiences and genuinely desire to develop others for a greater good. Leaders who are good mentors display patience, understanding, resourcefulness, generosity, and openness. They employ active listening skills, are adept at giving and receiving feedback and engaging in dialogue, and ask powerful questions and show empathy. They open up their networks, their minds, and their hearts to their mentees.

In addition, leaders who are good mentors are able to help the person they are mentoring define their leadership potential. These mentor-leaders fuel the fire of their own and their mentees' learning, and they support, nurture, and guide mentees to take a leadership role in their own careers and lives, making the mentee the master of his or her own goals.

Leaders are thoughtful about how they go about establishing successful mentoring relationships. They further realize that most professional mentoring relationships have four phases:

- Initiating
- Sustaining
- Producing
- Transitioning

Mentoring relationships are often started when a leader conveys openness and is approached by a mentee. However, a leader who is constantly looking for opportunities to grow and serve others will also identify and approach a potential mentee. Once the two parts of the dyad have found each other, their rapport and relationship begin to form around a central issue—the potential or need of the mentee.

The dyad frequently explores points of reference, views, and common interests as they build rapport. They determine individually if they can make the investment required for the relationship. Wise leaders move into the sustaining phase by mutually defining with the mentee what the goals, boundaries, roles, expectations, and outcomes of the relationship will be. They look for and define ways to best communicate and get their work and learning done.

The relationship expands to include more personal information from both the mentor and mentee—fears, failings, successes, or idiosyncrasies. It begins to evolve to a level of productivity in which the mentee is working on goals and the mentor is opening doors and guiding activities. As the leadership capacity of the mentee grows, the dyad transitions from an expert-novice relationship to that of colleague-colleague. The mentee begins to establish networks, taking on his or her own mentees, and becomes astute in determining what is needed for the next goal advancement.

The evolution of a mentee to this level of self-direction is a mentor's greatest success and satisfaction. Sometimes, the mentoring relationship ends here; other times, it is extended in a peer-peer relationship or friendship. The ultimate outcome of the relationship, however, is the growth and development of leaders.

The most influential mentor I have had in my life was my graduate school advisor. I didn't ask her to mentor me, she just took me on—seeing characteristics and potential in me that I did not. She continually challenged me to think and dig deeper for what my destiny was. Of course, we had goals that centered around my course of study and projects, but her powerful questions about the impact I wanted to make in nursing and the patient population I was serving left my head spinning at times. However, because of her probing, I began to define where I could make my best contribution.

She also gave me feedback—lots of it—which I now realize not only helped me form leadership skills in giving feedback myself, but also helped me plan, organize, and communicate more effectively. Lastly, by quizzing me about professional issues and trends and about my research studies, she taught me how to synthesize information and think quickly on my feet.

This mentor invested more time and energy in me than anyone else had. She opened her networks to me in our specialty area and watched without judgment as I made poor choices, but she was there to help me learn. This mentoring relationship went on intensely for two years. Two weeks before my graduation, she told me that I had the potential to be a national leader and make a difference for our profession. Two things happened with those words: She cut me loose to lead on my own, yet was there whenever I needed advice, support, or a friendly ear; and we moved from our expert-novice relationship to that of colleague-colleague.

Readiness and Reflections

1. Setting an example: Consider your daily behavior while reading each of the statements below and rate yourself as 1 (rarely do this), 2 (occasionally do this), or 3 (continually do this).

   _____ I am positive and optimistic.

   _____ I use stories, metaphors, and lived experiences to make my points.

   _____ I ask questions that require people to search for the meaning of their work.

   _____ I monitor my responses in work situations and wear my leader face.

   _____ I consider the consequences of my responses on others.

   _____ I am aware of the reactions of others to my words, deeds, and behaviors.

   _____ I am committed to learning and continuous improvement.

   _____ I tolerate failure and learn from it.

   _____ I am considered reliable, ethical, and respectful.

   _____ I am considered honest and fair.

   _____ I take responsibility for myself as well as my actions.

   _____ I demonstrate collaboration and teamwork.

2. For your "1" responses, create a plan of personal development. Seek the guidance of your own mentor.

3. Mentoring: While considering your daily behavior, read each of the following statements and rate yourself with 1 (rarely use this skill), 2 (frequently use this skill) or 3 (continuously use this skill).*

_____ I give full attention to others while listening.

_____ I listen for what is said and for underlying messages that are unsaid.

_____ I provide timely, specific, and constructive feedback.

_____ I compassionately help people realize how they limit themselves.

_____ I candidly share insider perspectives on how to navigate the work system effectively.

_____ I help people understand the politics and power dynamics behind issues.

_____ I regularly share my network and introduce people to those I know can assist them.

_____ I link people to professional organizations and resources that can help them.

_____ I ask questions that open up new perspectives.

_____ I value learning about myself and my potential.

_____ I help people connect their motivation, beliefs, and talents and focus on what they really want.

_____ I encourage people to stretch beyond their comfort zone and embrace challenges.

_____ I focus more on developing strengths than on repairing weaknesses.

_____ I honor people's freedom to choose how they want to be in the world.

_____ I brainstorm possibilities and explore options.

_____ I look for more than one right answer.

_____ I move other people and myself from talk to action.

_____ I focus people on making commitments to realize their goals.

Add up your score. Your overall assessment scores reflect how you actually use or demonstrate mentoring skills. The score can help you see where your strengths are and where improvements can be made.

1-18: Your desire to be a good mentor is strong. Before you take on the mentoring role, give yourself the opportunity to assess and build your leadership strengths and abilities, to examine your personal values and goals, and to determine what your purpose is in becoming a mentor. Share your discoveries with a peer or mentor as you continue to master mentoring.

19-37: You have many of the mentoring skills mastered. Identify ways to reinforce these and to help yourself stretch into areas that are less developed. Determine which areas need attention, and have a conversation with someone you respect who possesses the skills you wish to strengthen. Work with them to try out their strategies as you continue to master the art of mentoring.

38-54: Your mastery of mentoring is well advanced. As you continue to grow on your mentoring path, discover new strategies to expand your repertoire and continually connect with your talents and abilities.

*Adapted from: Klein, E. (2000). *Being a mentor in high fulfillment & performance at work: A career workshop.* Encinatas, CA: Wisdom Heart Press.

4. Make a list of the most influential leaders you have known. List what they specifically helped you with and what they gave you that made them so influential. Send each of them a note of appreciation.

5. Have a discussion with your team about mentoring, their beliefs about it, and their needs. Have each team member create a plan for securing and working with a mentor.

6. Reflect on past mentoring relationships you have had in which you were the mentor. How would your mentee describe your relationship? How did you make a difference in this mentee's leadership journey and development?

7. Reflect on what you have learned in this chapter and through the reflections on modeling and mentoring. Write a paragraph on where you see yourself today as a role model and mentor.

8. Develop two strategies to improve your modeling and mentoring competencies and add these to your personal leadership development plan.

Chapter 9

You Are Smarter Than I Am: Empowerment

"Leaders cannot give what is not theirs to give, so they create empowered environments that enable people to take responsibility for themselves, their work, and the organization."

Empowerment is not a present given by a generous leader. Empowerment is a choice people make, a gift they give themselves. Empowerment is about people gaining control over their lives, exercising freedom, and exerting autonomy. Leaders cannot give what is not theirs to give, so they create empowered environments that enable people to take responsibility for themselves, their work, and the organization.

Power Versus Authority

At the heart of empowerment is power—the capacity and potency to act. People who possess and use power have the option to make decisions and act on their own. Power transforms the choices one makes into actions and outcomes, eventually establishing autonomy.

Many of us have witnessed the evolution of autonomy in children learning to ride a bike, for example. Once the skill is mastered, the child has the capacity to ride all over the neighborhood. He or she can make decisions and act on his or her own. However, the child's choices are limited by parental authority—the parents' right to command or enforce obedience. Authority does not eliminate the child's power to make the decision; it limits the parameters. The child can still choose to ride the bike across the street to get to the park, even though the parent has placed a limitation on that power.

Power and authority usually go hand in hand, and the challenge for leaders, when working with people, is to achieve balance. Leaders want to build cultures or environments in which people take responsibility for themselves and the organization. They want to make others feel strong by enabling them to assume ownership for the group's success. They want to enhance the competence and confidence of others, so they can be actively engaged in reaching the vision.

Leaders do not want people blaming others or seeking control for control's sake. They want people to see themselves as forces for change and improvement. To do this, leaders have to share their power; they have to enable themselves to overcome habits and attitudes associated with power.

Shared Power

"Empowerment, however, does not mean unlimited permission to do whatever is desired. Empowerment is responsible freedom that ensures those closest to the issue have authority to make judgments and decisions on how an issue is handled."

The idea of a leader sharing power conjures up all sorts of mental images: The leader has no control, or the daily working of an organization or business runs amok. Empowerment, however, does not mean unlimited permission to do whatever is desired. Empowerment is responsible freedom that ensures those closest to the issue have authority to make judgments and decisions on how an issue is handled. An empowering environment is one in which people are responsible for creating a workplace they believe in (Block, 1996).

Empowerment

Grace was a staff nurse on a postsurgical unit who believed strongly in autonomous, evidence-based nursing practice supported by a shared-governance model. Her hospital had adopted this model, and she felt empowered by the system, policies, and procedures that were in place.

Grace had the power to make decisions about when patients were admitted to the floor, which allowed her to plan her work more efficiently. She had the authority to make decisions about patients' diets, mobility, and treatment schedules, allowing her to assess patients' needs, comfort, and timing considerations. She had authority to reach out for consultation or advice from multiple disciplines, allowing her to care for the patient in a holistic manner. Grace assessed patient response and progress and felt in control of how she delivered nursing care. By accepting the responsibilities of empowerment, she felt and showed more commitment, which was repeatedly noted by those she cared for.

The empowered environment comes from the leader's ability to shift control to the people doing the work. Leaders who share their power give people the opportunity to control their work and their destiny. When people feel they can determine their own way, and believe they have the resources and support needed to complete their work, they will persist and even go above and beyond to accomplish it (Kouzes & Posner, 2007). Without an empowered environment, there is little commitment to excel.

Leaders do exercise some degree of control in empowered environments; but this control, rather than being punitive or cautionary, emphasizes what is valued. In exercising control, leaders will spend time on situations, issues, and behaviors that achieve the desired results. Leaders will assign tasks or projects based on a person's interest or skill. They will define behaviors—such as cooperation and free information-sharing—that are important and acknowledge them. They will work with people to develop the interpersonal and decision-making skills needed to make judgments that are in the best interest of the group. In the empowered environment, leaders strengthen others to boost their confidence and performance, and to create a climate where people are involved.

 ## Power of a Group

Jill was director of nursing at a moderate-size urban hospital with 1,000 nurses. The hospital had had some troublesome years—there had been financial difficulties and a few high-profile mishaps. The image of the hospital, as well as the nursing care offered by the facility, was suffering.

Jill firmly believed in the need for the hospital in that community, as well as in the quality of care provided by that hospital. The administrators committed themselves to a new and improved facility, and Jill wanted the best nursing care in the city to be its calling card.

Jill knew she would need help from people smarter than she was to accomplish that goal. Her nurses were experienced, caring, and knowledgeable. She knew that, but she wasn't so sure others did, particularly the public.

Her first move was to convene her team of senior nurses and ask them for ideas and help in reaching the goal. The innovative ideas they offered were amazing, and she listened intently to everything they said. She recognized she had great talent on her staff, and together they weaved their shared vision into an image-building campaign.

Each nurse involved in the campaign had a role that suited his or her abilities. One worked with marketing to print and air ads about nursing in the hospital; another worked with information technology to regularly deliver all-staff messages about the nursing care; another polled the nurses to solicit patient care stories that would resonate with the community; and still another worked with human resources to develop a more robust nurse recognition program.

Team members took responsibility for creating and embodying the image they wanted to portray. They had 18 months to put the face of their hospital's nursing on the city map and were committed to accomplishing this goal.

The campaign was an arduous process that encountered many challenges. Jill and her team supported one another and learned from their mistakes. They made decisions and built partnerships and alliances. They challenged and asked questions. They shared information and put the team first. At about the 18-month mark, things were beginning to improve for the hospital. The patient census was up, as were services. The financial picture had improved, and no further alarming patient events had occurred. As she walked around, Jill also noticed that the tone and atmosphere in the hospital were more upbeat, particularly among the nurses.

Over the course of the next 3 years, Jill monitored data that measured public perception of nursing care at the hospital. Consistently, nurses from that institution were among the top three in the city. The image-building campaign was working. Jill received many accolades for her strategy but, like a true leader, she demurred and recognized the group effort. In the end, what made the campaign so successful was Jill's ability to step back and share her power in pursuit of a higher purpose.

Reaching Empowered Environments

Like leadership, empowerment is a never-ending journey, one that requires continual diligence, patience, learning, and trust. Wise leaders make the investment in responsible freedom, knowing the end result is people who are happier and more vested contribute significantly to the leader's vision. Leaders overcome the pitfalls of empowerment, such as people who are overzealous and make decisions without the experience or competence needed, or people who are content to just do as they are told. Leaders do this because of the difference it makes to them and the people they work with (Bell & Bell, 2003).

Reaching empowered environments is all about how the leader makes people feel. It is about being clear about what is to be accomplished, what the parameters are for getting it done, and how support and resources can be provided so the team can succeed. Leaders build confidence and engage others in ownership and decision-making.

Engage in Ownership

People are more committed, and work harder, when they feel they are part of an important cause. Leaders who create, with others, the vision for this cause are asking them to take ownership of the endeavor. When leaders share power with others, they are asking them to make responsible decisions on behalf of the cause. Engagement in ownership begins and ends with the leader's ability to provide focus, so that each person feels he or she owns a piece of the puzzle. Each person becomes his or her own cottage industry in pursuing the purpose.

For example, when asked, "What are you working on today?" an apathetic nurse may say, "I am giving medications." In contrast, the committed nurse will say, "I am caring for these patients so they can get well and go home." Empowered environments enable people to own their work. Leaders create such environments through permission-giving and delegation.

Owning one's work and being empowered involve parameters. Leaders do not give power away with an unlimited license to make decisions and act. Rather, they establish clear expectations as to timelines and results, and they define limitations to the power given. Within the guidelines established, the person is liberated to use his or her own power to get the job done.

A clinical nurse specialist wanted to implement a new evidence-based practice on her unit. She presented the practice to her leader, who found merit in its implications for patient recovery time. The leader gave permission, support, and power to the clinical nurse specialist to make decisions as the practice was being implemented, but she placed limitations on the implementation. For example, she required evidence of uptake of the practice in 6 months; the nurse specialist's regular patient responsibilities had to be met; and refusal by the patient had to be honored.

Over the course of the implementation, the nurse specialist made her own decisions about which nursing staff to enlist as change champions, the communication that was shared, and what to do in the event of problems with the patient. She took ownership of the practice and its implementation.

Part of being a great leader lies in recognizing that one does not know—nor can one do—everything that needs to happen to reach a vision. Thus, leaders are constantly looking for people more talented and competent than they are. Once they find the right people with the right talent mix, leaders assign responsibility and authority to those people to get the job completed. When leaders delegate, they are empowering others—freeing them to act, make decisions, issue orders, and be responsible. But delegation is a lot of hard work.

How many times have you had a chance to receive help with a task and thought, "It is just easier to do it myself." In doing so, leaders shortchange themselves and their followers, because they are wasting valuable talent, including their own.

As a CEO, I was responsible for the annual budget preparation. While I was adept in this skill, I delegated it to the controller, giving him full authority to direct the work with the budget managers and to make decisions about line items. My expectations were the completion of a positive budget with detailed revenue and expenditure notes by a certain date. In delegating, I deployed his talents and competency for the good of the organization and freed my time to build business partnerships that benefited our vision. Delegation should be a win-win situation for leaders, followers, and the people they serve.

 ## Successful Delegation

Mind Tools (2008) offers 10 easy principles to follow for successful delegation:

1. Articulate the desired outcome clearly.
2. Identify constraints and boundaries.
3. Include those affected in the delegation process.

4. Match the amount of responsibility with the amount of authority.

5. Delegate to the people who are closest to the work.

6. Provide adequate support and resources.

7. Focus on results; let the results determine the way.

8. Ask for solutions when problems are encountered, rather than providing solutions.

9. Relate tasks to the common good.

10. Provide guidelines, timelines, and recognition when deserved.

Engage in Competence and Confidence-Building

If the environment is truly empowered, people will feel the leader takes an interest in them personally and professionally. They believe the leader wants them to succeed as they work toward the vision. For this reason, opinions count to leaders. Leaders who want to create a climate in which people personally have a stake go out of their way to learn what others are thinking. They encourage people to see themselves as having the influence to improve their work and life. Leaders want people to think on their own, using creativity to act and decide for the organization.

To promote autonomy, the leader must be open and broad-minded. Leaders who want to share their power with others must be willing to open themselves up to possibilities and think about things differently. Frequently, the empowering leader will ask, "What is working well for you? What is not?" These questions convey the leader's interest to the person and provide an opportunity to brainstorm. For the leader, the questions provide a gauge of efficiency and a chance to listen to ideas from the person doing the work.

Being broad-minded expands one's knowledge base and provides more information with which to make decisions. Leaders provide people with the chance to ask questions, learn, and share thoughts in an empowered environment. This atmosphere stimulates knowledge-sharing and, with experience, results in wisdom that can be deployed to fulfill the vision.

Leaders who empower are also fair-minded. This becomes quite clear when a person makes a mistake. The leader who believes in an empowering environment will see the mistake as an opportunity to learn, coach, and problem-solve, rather than rebuke. Empowerment is risky, but without risk there is no creativity or learning. Along with risk come honest mistakes. Empowerment is trusting—the greater the risk, the greater the trust and, frequently, the greater the freedom to choose and decide. And, the more freedom a person has, the greater the responsibility. Leaders want people to become increasingly comfortable and competent with more and more responsibility (Bell & Bell, 2003).

Confidence influences everyone's ability to function successfully. It gives people motivation to take on tough challenges and push themselves. Leaders build the self-confidence of others by supporting their decisions and by telling them when they do a good job. In fostering self-confidence, leaders help people build inner strength and extend themselves. One of the most important things leaders can express is their belief in the ability of others to succeed.

Engage in Decision-Making

Leaders use a wide variety of decision-making styles, but wise leaders and their teams participate in any style of decision-making with equal skill and talent. Some decisions require a group approach, others a top-down method. For some decisions, the leader wants input only; for others, the leader tells the team or person to make the decision. Regardless of the style and method, the most important thing about decision-making is to decide *how* you are going to decide (Winters & Klein, 2004).

Leaders who grow empowered environments know that engaging people in decision-making can increase not only participation and commitment, but the quality of the decision's outcome as well. Leaders who share their power and give decision-making authority to others gain greater organizational effectiveness and higher performance (Kouzes & Posner, 2007).

This phenomenon of the more power you give away, the more powerful you become occurs because, in sharing their power, leaders are showing profound trust and respect for others' abilities. "When leaders help others grow and develop, that help is reciprocated. People who feel capable of influencing their leaders are more strongly attached to those leaders and more committed to effectively carrying out their responsibilities. They own their jobs" (Kouzes & Posner, 2007, p. 287). Giving authority to people to do their jobs is one of the most effective empowering methods a leader can use.

Coupled with sharing decision-making authority, leaders provide resources and support that bolster the authority given—the proverbial "put your money where your mouth is." It is one thing to listen to someone's idea, and quite another to step back and help them act on the idea. Great leaders do just that: They help people turn their ideas into decisions with authority.

In supporting those decisions, the leader gives people the opportunity to feel personal effectiveness. This "can-do" feeling encourages them to expand themselves and do whatever is needed to reach the goals and vision. In liberating the leader within each person, the leader gives people the tools—power and authority—to use the skills and talents they already have. They provide people with the chance to expand their opportunities and create meaning in their work.

In this age of rapidly changing work environments, nimbleness is essential. Only adaptive people and organizations will thrive in the future. Leaders have to provide increasing levels of choice by sharing their power and influence. This ability to create empowered environments that use and expand the talents of others is a hallmark of a great leader.

A Nurse Who Empowered Her Patients' Environment

Angie was a nurse practitioner in a breast-cancer clinic. She cared for patients who were newly diagnosed and in treatment, and also for survivors of breast cancer. One of Angie's many talents was the ability to make the patient feel like she was the only person in the world who mattered when Angie was with her. She also possessed an amazing, up-to-date knowledge base about breast cancer and its diagnosis, treatment, and prognosis.

I had the pleasure of meeting and getting to know Angie when I accompanied a friend to appointments following the friend's diagnosis of breast cancer. Angie had actually found the tumor when my friend went to the breast cancer center for a routine examination and mammogram.

On this particular visit, my friend was learning about her treatment options. Angie handled these visits before sending the patient to surgeons, oncologists, and radiologists for treatment. Why she handled these visits became abundantly clear after 5 minutes with her. Angie spoke with patients at this juncture in their illness because her job was to educate, inform, support, and unlock the person's inner strength to make decisions about the best course of treatment. She was not there to prescribe, recommend, or tell my friend what to do.

During our visit, Angie openly shared information with my friend. She was honest about the type of cancer that was isolated on the biopsy and the likelihood of other tissue being involved. She prodded my friend to ask questions and encouraged her to express her emotions. Angie was quite respectful of the upheaval my friend was experiencing. Many times, Angie asked if my friend would like to break up our visit into several visits.

With my friend's permission, Angie told her she had several decisions to make, and only she had the authority to make them. Angie told my friend that she needed to hear and consider her options, which Angie explained in a most scientific, organized, and knowledgeable way. This approach appealed to my friend, who is a no-nonsense, give-it-to-me-straight person. Angie recognized this about her and tailored her approach accordingly.

Angie also recognized my friend's need to discuss options with those close to her and encouraged her to do so. She provided her personal phone number, so my friend could consult and talk with her. Angie was clearly empowering my friend with information and authority to make decisions—to exercise power over her life. In fact, my friend said it best later that day, "For having received the worst news of my life today, I feel remarkably in control of what will happen." Angie is the kind of leader who creates empowered environments for her patients.

Readiness and Reflection

1. *Rate yourself on a scale of 1 to 5, with 1 indicating you do this sometimes and 5 indicating you do this nearly all the time. As a leader, I build empowered environments because:

   _____ I share information openly.

   _____ I invest time in building group consensus.

   _____ I delegate power and authority.

   _____ I encourage inquiry and questioning.

   _____ I seek to understand the point of view of others.

   _____ I actively seek the opinions of others.

   _____ I provide guidelines for making decisions.

   _____ I encourage people to be responsible for their own decisions.

   _____ I provide opportunities to build existing and new talents and skills.

   _____ I let people assume ownership of their work.

   _____ I make thoughtful and informed decisions.

   _____ I practice and expect autonomy.

   _____ I learn from mistakes.

   _____ I work to improve.

   _____ I treat people with respect and dignity.

   Add up your score. If you scored 51-75, you are well on your way to being an empowered leader. As this is a continual journey, keep paying attention to those behaviors and skills that make people feel free to do their work with purpose.

   If your score is 26-50, you are moving in the right direction. Examine those skills where you scored the lowest, and develop a tactic or two for improvement. Internalizing shared power and decision-making takes a lot of hard work and practice.

If you scored 1-25, you have some strong skills, but others that need work. Start working on one skill a month, and build your repertoire over time.

* Adapted from Hutson, D. (2002). *Best practices of empowering leaders.* Retrieved August 4, 2008, from http://www.frogpond.com

2. With your team, have a discussion about power, what it means to each member, and what behaviors demonstrate it. Start the discussion by asking each person to list three words that immediately come to mind when you say the word "power." End the discussion with asking each person what the source of their personal power is and how it helps them meet their responsibilities.

3. Ask the people who work with and for you to tell you two ways they do not feel empowered by the environment. Discuss how this could be changed to make them feel more in control.

4. Develop a Power Profile (Kouzes & Posner, 2002, pp. 83-84) for each member of your team. In the profile, list:

   - which strength is most useful to the team
   - what that member's unique perspective is
   - what education or support he or she needs to become strong
   - what opportunities you can provide to increase the member's responsible freedom
   - what information the person needs to be productive
   - what team opportunities you can provide the person.

5. For each person, identify one action you can take to increase his or her competence and confidence. Evaluate progress in 1 month.

6. Consider a time when you felt powerful in your work. Write down what you were doing and what your leader did to create the environment in which you felt powerful. Now, consider a time when you felt powerless. What was the difference in the environment between the powerless and the powerful times?

7. Reflect on what you have learned about empowerment from this chapter and the exercises. Write one paragraph about where you see yourself today as an empowering leader.

8. Develop two strategies to improve your empowerment skills, and add them to your personal leadership development plan.

Chapter 10

Is This In My Job Description?
Accountability and Transparency

Let us pause for a moment and consider the leadership journey so far. Leaders are ordinary people who have strong values and beliefs. They are clear about their purpose in life and work. Their journey starts with self-discovery, awareness, and discipline that find expression in living according to their values. Leaders are self-confident, and they extend this confidence to others who are inspired to join them in making a difference that achieves a greater good.

Leaders earn the trust of those around them because of their integrity. They align their words and behaviors with their values, and they exhibit a passion for their cause that is infectious. Leaders believe in the future of possibilities, and they create compelling visions around them. But they know the vision is not theirs alone if truly great things are to happen. They ask others to share in creating and living the vision, doing so with a healthy dose of reality. Leaders motivate and inspire by enlisting and actively involving others to join in achieving the vision.

Leaders use a potpourri of communication and listening talents to keep people engaged and working toward the vision. They also model and mentor them to realize their full potential and contribution toward the greater good. As they move themselves and others

> "Leaders earn the trust of those around them because of their integrity. They align their words and behaviors with their values, and they exhibit a passion for their cause that is infectious."

along the leadership road, leaders engage in continuous learning and improvement. They also share their power and authority with others, supporting and teaching them to be leaders themselves. Along the way, leaders set up systems, structures, processes, and guidelines to support fulfillment of their vision, and throughout the journey, they accept accountability for doing the right thing. The shared vision, shared power, and shared values all carry a price. If they are to be fulfilled, someone has to be responsible for making it happen. That someone is the leader.

Accountability

Accountability—the responsibility and authority to act, fully accepting the consequences of those actions—is unavoidable (Willard & Hitchcock, 2008). Many people aspire to be leaders, but few are prepared to accept the accountability that goes hand-in-hand with being a leader. Most people think of accountability as a top-down phenomenon. While it is true that senior leaders and executives hold accountability for what transpires overall, one person's accountability does not create a culture of accountability. This culture can only develop when all accept accountability to act responsibly for the common good.

In an empowered environment, where leaders share their vision and power with others, accountability becomes part of the equation and job description. Leaders recognize that when people take responsibility for their actions—whether good or bad—they become more trusting and cooperative. Interconnectedness among people occurs when they are confident that, if one person does his part, others will do theirs.

For example, when a patient-care team comes together for a shift, each team member has functions that must be completed. The leader assigns tasks based on the individual's competency and skill to do the work. Perhaps one is responsible for personal care, another for treatments and medications, and still another for assessment and coordination. Each team member is trusted and works in cooperation with others to deliver good patient care. In fulfilling assigned responsibilities, team members are accountable to themselves, their colleagues, and the patient.

The Three-Legged Accountability Stool

Leaders understand that they must develop accountability systems while keeping three principles in mind: focus, influence, and consequences (Willard & Hitchcock, 2008). To achieve an organization that is accountable, each of these components must be balanced with the others.

Clarity of focus and expectations is the basis for a system of accountability. The leader helps the team establish a clear goal statement that is directly related to the vision. The leader permits the group to develop its own identity, outcomes, and ways of work that are congruent with those of the leader and organization. The leader also encourages each person in the group to identify his or her specific talents that may contribute to the group's success.

As groups begin their work together, leaders vest them with the power to influence how they perform their work, as well as how they influence each other. Individuals in the group must have authority to influence each other's behavior. Only through this empowerment can the group influence its collective effort.

For example, if the group includes a slacker who allows others to do tasks for him or her, the group as a whole must have authority to address the issue. As a rule, slackers generally step up to meet the challenge and responsibility when confronted with their behavior. However, the group must have the power to remove that person if his or her performance is detrimental to the group. Leaders know they must set up conditions that enable each group to feel a sense of ownership and accountability for the entire job.

Leaders further understand that, if accountability is to be taken seriously, the system must include consequences for unsatisfactory performance. Such mechanisms require that the group or person handle the situation, rather than take it to the boss for resolution.

Leaders also establish performance and compensation measures that link the whole group's performance to individual performance. For example, if the goal of a nursing-care team is to reduce incidence of pressure sores to less than 1 percent of patients on the unit, this goal is measured for all who work together on the unit. If the team fails to meet the goal, the performance of individuals must be corrected. This is as much the group's responsibility as it is the manager's.

Levels of Accountability

Three basic levels of accountability are needed: personal, group, and culture. With personal accountability, each person feels a deep sense of commitment and responsibility for the group's work. This sense results from valuing the work and the people doing it. Each person understands assigned responsibilities and clearly sees his or her contribution. With personal accountability, the individual feels ownership and is ready to see things through to completion. People can deal with the consequences when they feel valued and obligated to contribute.

Group accountability, where most of us function and lead, connects personal accountabilities into an interdependent matrix. Individuals with their personal accountabilities come together in groups to work collaboratively. This effort has a goal or mission that is related to the larger vision, and the group defines its purpose around this mission.

"With personal accountability, each person feels a deep sense of commitment and responsibility for the group's work."

For example, the technology department of an organization is composed of programmers, designers, hardware and software specialists, and perhaps scientists and information architects. Their mission is to provide seamless technology service to the organization. Each has personal accountability to get the assigned job done, knowing that if he or she doesn't follow through, others will be impaired in getting their jobs done.

If the software person lets a virus disrupt service, then the programmers and designers are unable to their work. If the programmers shut the system down for too long while putting in new computing codes, others are unable to do their work. The unsatisfactory performance of one influences the performance of others and the organization as a whole. Each person must do his or her part for the group to function effectively.

Leaders structure environments so that people have to work collaboratively, because collaborative work increases personal accountability (Kouzes & Posner, 2002). People who are committed do not want to let the rest of the group down. They want to do their best, because they know the group is expecting them to do so. The pressure of peers and the desire to be placed in a favorable light are powerful motivators. Therefore, group members will hold each other accountable, ensuring full participation.

A culture of accountability is established when group accountability permeates an organization. Groups are viewed as singular entities, and each person in the group answers for the group's action. The focus is on the total group effort, not on how one person or another contributes.

As groups function with accountability across an organization, a culture of responsibility forms. For example, in an organization that develops continuing education for nurses, there might be several groups: content developers, promotional staff to market the offerings, administrative staff to register people, logistical staff to make classroom arrangements, technology staff to create tracking infrastructures, and financial staff to monitor fiscal value. Each group has accountability to the end result: well-received, value-added continuing education content for professionals.

Each person has responsibility to do his or her job well, because others depend on it. Each group has the influence and authority to achieve expected results, and willingly accepts the consequences for its actions. When the program is offered and is deemed a success, the organization and its groups experience enhanced desire to work harder.

"When mistakes are openly embraced as learning opportunities, people are more willing to admit to them and find solutions."

But what if the results fall short of expected outcomes? This is the tough part of accountability, because the biggest fear of individuals and groups is punishment. Effective leaders realize that placing blame, rather than focusing on finding solutions, is harmful. Blame and punishment create victim mentalities and secretive cultures in which people act individually in their own best interest, rather than for the group's best interest.

Successful organizations that have a culture of accountability actually celebrate mistakes as learning opportunities. Leaders focus on figuring out how to do things differently, rather than finger-pointing. Some groups hold weekly or monthly meetings to discuss their biggest blunders. This approach not only brings problems to the surface, it solves them. It also drives fear away (Willard & Hitchcock, 2008).

"Successful organizations that have a culture of accountability actually celebrate mistakes as learning opportunities."

What is to be feared when people are honestly discussing their mess-ups and looking for ways to avoid them in the future? When mistakes are openly embraced as learning opportunities, people are more willing to admit to them and find solutions.

Transparency

In a discussion about transparency, a leader was asked if transparency meant the person was invisible. Transparency to the questioner meant one could see right through a person, as if he or she were not there. The group laughed softly at the question, perhaps because they, too, thought it meant the same thing. The leader replied, "No, transparency does not mean you are invisible, but it does mean people can see through you." This reply raised additional questions. "We don't get it," they said. The leader replied, "Transparency means your actions, communications, and behaviors are so open, frank, and freely available that others understand immediately what you stand for and are doing."

Transparency is the opposite of privacy. It encompasses the ability of others to easily detect and recognize what a person is doing. For example, the leader who hoards reports and does not share them with others is easily recognized as an information tyrant. Or, the person who readily points the finger in blame when things go wrong is readily identified as a team foe, rather than a colleague.

On the other hand, the leader who willingly shares financial statements and organizational action plans is seen as one who is open and candid. Or, the person who holds open meetings to brainstorm a new idea is recognized as collegial and inclusive in decision-making. Transparency is the means to achieve an environment of accountability.

The concept of transparency was introduced as a means for fighting corruption and holding public officials accountable. Leaders are seen as transparent when government meetings are open to the public and press, budgets and financial statements may be reviewed by anyone, and rules and decisions are open to discussion. There is also less opportunity for them to abuse the system or organization in their own interest.

Over time, the principle and practices of transparency have found their way into businesses, organizations, and communities as a moral compass for behavior. Increasingly, leaders understand the importance of never pretending to be someone they are not by overstepping the boundaries and doing something that is not in the best interest of their organization.

"Transparency is the opposite of privacy. It encompasses the ability of others to easily detect and recognize what a person is doing."

Transparency allows the leader to create, every day, an opportunity for others to participate in the vision-work at hand. If leaders are going to share their vision and power with others, it is in their best interest to be as open and frank, or transparent, as possible. Transparency further enables people around the leader to work on goals in an atmosphere of trust.

Not all information and decisions are open, however, and the leader has to continually balance the need for confidentiality with the need for sharing information. For example, a leader might not share information about personal or professional issues of one group member with the others. Or, most leaders choose not to share compensation information publically across groups. The key in these circumstances is that the leader be open and frank about his or her inability to share confidential information, thus demonstrating transparency.

While complete transparency is not possible, leaders do develop a sense of what and how much information people can handle. Given the vast amounts and speed of information flow in current environments, leaders face this challenge daily. They gauge the amount of input people can tolerate and learn when to turn up the heat on information flow and decisions and when to lower it. They derive their ability to do this from their purpose and belief in doing the right thing. It takes courage and communication to know how to be transparent while maintaining an honorable, caring, and respectful style.

Accountability in Action

 ## A Culture of Accountability

When Diane assumed the position of associate dean for academic affairs at a large state university school of nursing, her challenge was to transform seven department directors in the undergraduate program into a cohesive, cooperative group of faculty members. The directors were frequently at odds and pushed the job of educating students on each other. In the end, this group developed a set of guidelines for how they would work and communicate. Included in these guidelines were decision-making and problem-solving processes, behavioral norms, responsibility statements, definition of consequences, and a mission statement.

Department directors received a copy of the guidelines and signed a statement accepting them as a contract of how they would perform their work. In turn, each director discussed the guidelines with his or her respective faculty members, who also signed the contract. After years of working together in a disgruntled manner, the group of seven became a cohesive team that focused on educating students and working collaboratively across the departments. Eventually, this culture of working together permeated most of the department faculty. But this did not occur overnight, and Diane began by making the seven directors accountable, implementing the process that follows.

She brought the directors together and laid out a proposal for them to own their own departments, giving them power and authority to make decisions. Diane was quite clear about the outcomes she expected and emphasized that the authority and responsibility to optimize student education, scheduling, and success were theirs.

That first meeting quickly got out of hand and became a gripe session laced with blaming. Diane was patient with them, recognizing this was probably the first time they were all in the room together and able to speak freely. When they realized that Diane was intent on making them full participants and decision-makers, they warmed to the idea and began to participate.

Over the course of several months, Diane worked beside them as they developed and began to own their guidelines. In fact, the directors actually looked forward to the meetings and were beginning to develop camaraderie. The hardest part came when the discussion rolled around to consequences. No one wanted to be that accountable! But Diane pushed the concept, gave them examples of what others had used, and encouraged them to focus on what was best for the school and individual students, rather than what they regarded as their personal entitlements.

Diane was sure the whole process was going to blow up when she asked them to write their own mission statements and goals. But as they shared them with each other, a new sense of purpose evolved, allowing them to see the kind of graduate they wanted to produce. They saw how each of them contributed to this student's eventual ability to be the kind of nurse they envisioned. The directors recognized that, by working together more cohesively, they could accomplish more than by working alone or at cross-purposes. They also realized they had wasted energy and valuable resources by working in protected silos.

Diane continued to meet regularly with the directors as they implemented a culture of accountability with the faculty members who reported to them. She continually reinforced their awareness of accountability by recognizing the success of individual directors in the presence of their peers. This reinforced the feeling of strength and capability of both the group and individual members. Accountability of counterparts and a job well done result in feelings of ownership that we—not someone else—have responsibility for what happens around us.

Readiness and Reflection

1. Reflecting on your accountability behaviors, answer yes or no to the following statements. To promote accountability:

_____ I require groups to define their purpose and outcomes.

_____ I have groups define each member's role and responsibilities.

_____ I have groups establish clear standards and guidelines for their work.

_____ I require groups to track and analyze their own performance data.

_____ I invite others to participate in shaping vision and mission.

_____ I use performance feedback for problem solving.

_____ I ask groups to analyze work practices for improvement.

_____ I give groups authority for budgets and decisions.

_____ I require groups to regularly give each other feedback.

_____ I give groups authority to select and remove members.

_____ I link rewards and compensation to team outcomes.

_____ I define consequences for nonacceptable behaviors.

_____ I use "I" sentences, avoiding blaming and excuses.

_____ I am specific about how decisions are linked to mission and results.

_____ I accept responsibility for mistakes.

_____ I turn errors into learning opportunities.

For all "no" responses, consider and implement two tactics to shift them to "yes."

2. Write two paragraphs about your personal accountability. What would you change? What is working well?

3. Make a list of the ways you demonstrate and promote accountability on a daily basis.

4. Reflect on an accountability situation that was difficult for you. What made it so difficult? How would you have handled it differently?

5. Have a retreat with your team and make accountability its focus. Set a goal to develop a team contract for how you will work together, and complete it at the retreat. Have team members sign the contract within two weeks of the retreat.

6. Reflect on what you have read in this chapter and your responses to the exercises. Write a paragraph on where you see yourself as an accountable, transparent leader.

7. Develop two strategies to improve your accountability and transparency skills, and add them to your personal leadership development plan.

Chapter 11

Change Is My Middle Name: Being an Agent of Change

Change is a way of life. Whether it is varying your commute to work because of construction or altering your job responsibilities because of reorganization, change is part of our lives every day.

One of the major differences between managers and leaders is that managers cope with complexity in fulfilling their responsibilities, while leaders cope with change. Without good management, complex organizations cannot function effectively and efficiently. Good management brings order and consistency to the work of an enterprise. Leadership, on the other hand, brings vision, purpose, and direction to the ever-changing world of work. Without good leadership, organizations become chaotic and miss opportunities to thrive and excel. The more change there is, the more good leadership is needed (Kotter, 2002).

While leadership and management complement each other, each is distinct in its function, and both are needed to achieve success. As previously discussed, leaders set the direction, align people, and motivate and enable them. Managers plan and budget, control, problem-solve, and organize.

"Without good leadership, organizations become chaotic and miss opportunities to thrive and excel."

Myatt (2007) describes leaders as very creative, dynamic, outgoing, and unflappable individuals. Leaders tend to think "big picture," focusing on vision and strategy while looking for long-term impact. They embrace change and risk. Managers, on the other hand, are usually more analytic; they focus on policy and procedure, looking to make short-term contributions. They prefer comfort and control and are operationally bound. Both leaders and managers bring these key competencies to the table to create the banquet of success. However, it is the leader's responsibility to consistently seek out opportunity, determine direction, and guide change. Leaders of the future are change-ready and change-savvy.

Understanding Change and Its Impact

Change is inherently, and unavoidably, an emotional human process. Whether it occurs in our personal, professional, or organizational life, change is about relinquishing something, and this loss creates emotional response. In *The Change Monster*, author Jeanie Duck describes this response to change as the change monster: "a catch-all phrase for the complex, often scary, human emotions and social dynamics that emerge like a dragon surfacing from the ocean depths during any major change effort" (Duck, p. xi, 2001). Like other emotions or dynamics in life, change can be managed effectively to achieve positive, desired results.

Response to change plays out in four distinct phases: denial, resistance, exploration, and commitment.

"Whether it occurs in our personal, professional, or organizational life, change is about relinquishing something, and this loss creates emotional response."

In the *denial* phase, the reaction to change is to refuse to recognize the information. Common responses are: This can't be happening; it will pass; or this is just a minor adjustment. People can work in the denial phase but, sooner or later, the impact of change hits home, and a personal response is required.

Each individual affected by a change can choose to control or not control his or her response and behavior. But, in responding to change, people must figure out *what* the change means for their values and beliefs, and determine *if* they can live and function within the shifted paradigm. Then they must figure out *how* they are going to do this.

This period of discovery is especially important for the leader. If the leader cannot model adaptation to change, others cannot find the new meaning and be expected to follow. For everyone who is impacted by change, self-change must occur and, with self-change, emotions flourish.

"If the leader cannot model adaptation to change, others cannot find the new meaning and be expected to follow."

We have all experienced the roller coaster of change—its pain, uncertainty, chaos, calm, and jubilation. We have all seen, and perhaps displayed, the predictable emotions associated with change, ranging from fear, rage, resistance, and grief to relief, curiosity, delight, and optimism.

Resistance is the second phase in responding to change. In this phase, the situation seems to get worse. Personal distress rises as the change becomes a reality. Emotions run deep and physical and mental symptoms sometimes occur. Individuals are forced to acknowledge their feelings and begin to recognize their choices.

Leaders recognize that emotions are data. They read the emotions, analyze them, and give them voice, knowing that doing so is critical for any change initiative to succeed. The leader allows time and space for emotions, addressing the intellectual and emotional aspects of the change, as well as the operational and system aspects.

Change requires people to think and act differently. After a period of struggle in responding to change, individuals generally enter the third phase—*exploration*. What first emerges is energy to search out and explore new ways. Individuals start clarifying goals, assessing resources, exploring alternatives, and experimenting with new possibilities. Creativity and energy peak, and people begin to see what the change means to them. People begin to self-lead.

During this phase, leaders step up the urgency of action and start building a team to guide the change. This team of allies is critical to successful change, as it assumes responsibility for mobilizing commitment and creating a shared vision for the new paradigm. Leaders are often among the first to embrace changes, and they help others adjust to new ways of thinking.

During exploration, leaders clearly and repeatedly communicate the change vision. They coach and facilitate their change team and others. They empower others to act, grant power and authority, and remove barriers. Leaders frequently revisit goals and expectations, recognize contributions, and celebrate small wins along the way. As individuals and teams experience these initial successes, they move into the final phase of responding to change—commitment and determination.

> *"During exploration, leaders clearly and repeatedly communicate the change vision."*

During this phase, people begin to focus on the new course of action and ways of work. This might be reflected as a new set of responsibilities or a new way of doing the same responsibilities. The key here is that individuals are adapting to the new situation and demonstrate willingness to move on from old ways. Acknowledgement is extremely important in this phase, and leaders celebrate successes to build momentum and enthusiasm.

Leaders also recognize that it is important not to rest once commitment is demonstrated. Deflation and complacency can happen quickly during this phase, so leaders use it as a time to learn, grow, and seek new ways to do things even better in the new paradigm. This strategy sustains the change and enables new and winning behaviors.

 ## A Story of Change

Becky was an emergency department nurse manager who worked the evening shift. She was extremely competent and enjoyed her position at a major city hospital. Becky was frustrated, however, by what she perceived as ineffectiveness and slackness of others in her department. She was routinely aggressive, outspoken, and critical of her co-workers, sometimes in private and others times openly in meetings. Her reputation with her patients was superb, but her co-workers considered her someone to steer clear of.

Finally, one of Becky's friends decided to confront her with the truth—she was the source of friction and stress in the department.

The friend gently, but firmly, told Becky that her style was causing her harm and lowering morale in the department. She explained that if Becky wanted to create department policy and procedure change for the patients, she first needed to make some personal changes.

At first, Becky was hurt and angry about her friend's comments, but after calming down, she began to seriously reflect on her behavior. She sought out a mentor and acquired training on resolving conflicts and working as a team member. Slowly, but surely, Becky began to practice what she had learned. Her behavior changed, and so did people's response to her. She discovered others were more open to her suggestions and questions. Her opinion was sought more frequently, and she even learned to laugh at herself when old behaviors would creep in. She experienced a behavior and mind-set change that allowed her to be a leader for the department.

Being a Risk Taker

Seldom does something of significance happen without some measure of risk-taking. Risk is literally defined in a negative sense—the chance of harm, injury, or danger. For the leader, however, risk is defined as the chance to do things in new ways, to experiment with innovation.

Risk is a bit of a paradox for most of us. We are continually looking for something new or original, yet are uncomfortable about trying something different. However, risk-taking is an essential part of leadership and is evidenced by courage to try new ways, even when the outcome is uncertain and things are going poorly (Matusak, 1997).

Leaders take risks every day by stepping forward, speaking out, and putting themselves in situations that are not totally secure. Simply put, leaders try new things, recognizing that more is gained from taking an action that fails than from taking no action at all. Leaders who take risks must have the courage to stretch beyond their comfort zones. Stretching limits strengthens leaders even if they fail, because in the process, they learn about ways they can improve.

"Simply put, leaders try new things, recognizing that more is gained from taking an action that fails than from taking no action at all."

Moving into areas that are beyond our limits and capacities may seem foolish to some and, indeed, produces anxiety and fear. Leaders, however, display confidence when taking a chance, because they believe it is the right thing to do to reach the vision. Leaders regard risk-taking as a calculated, conscious decision to do something they are not sure will work. They dare to follow their vision with their eyes open (Mahlmeister, 2000). They overcome fear of failure and concern for what others may think, because they know that too much caution delays the decision and frequently means lost opportunity.

Leaders are able to move into action as opportunities present themselves by practicing the three essentials of risk-taking: initiate incremental steps and small wins, learn from mistakes, and promote psychological hardiness (Kouzes & Posner, 2007).

Change Processes

The most effective change processes are incremental. Leaders break the larger problem or issue into small, achievable steps with distinct objectives and milestones. While keeping the vision in clear sight, leaders repeatedly persuade people to say yes and take one step at a time toward the goal.

First, leaders begin with actions that are doable and within their control. Knowing that followers must see progress, leaders build commitment by celebrating small wins. For example, an advanced practice nurse who had administrative authority over nursing in a primary-care center wanted to implement evidence-based practice. She believed this practice model would benefit patients and nurses by providing care with the most up-to-date research knowledge. Rather than delivering a mandate to implement this model throughout the center, she selected one health care issue and, with a team of allies, developed a pilot protocol for care.

All the nurses, from the triage nurse to the practitioner seeing the patient, used the evidence-based protocol for 60 days. When the nurses realized that their assessments and advice were more accurate and better-received by patients, and produced improved health results, they were willing to say yes to implementing additional protocols.

This commitment increased even more when the administrator began posting the statistical results of their protocol implementation and recognized the nurses who achieved the results. Step by step, the administrator developed new protocols and enlisted other nurses to develop them. Fairly soon, the nurses were coming up with their own evidence-based innovations and, after 10 months, the model was integrated into nursing practice throughout the center.

> *"Research has repeatedly shown that leaders regard mistakes and failures as essential to success."*

Learning From Failure

Mistakes and failures are bound to happen when taking risks, and they can be costly. The cost might be to one's pride, the company's bottom line, or to a personal career, but research has repeatedly shown that leaders regard mistakes and failures as essential to success (Kotter, 2002; Kouzes & Posner, 2007). There is benefit from learning and doing it again, only better.

Abraham Lincoln failed in business twice and was defeated in six elections before being elected president. Babe Ruth struck out more than 1,300 times, but between his strikeouts, he set a record of 714 home runs. Nothing ever happens perfectly the first, second, or even 10th time, but if people don't learn from failure, they will keep making the same mistakes. Leaders don't advocate failure, but they do support learning from a failed experiment.

Leaders are aware that the only way people can learn is by doing things they have never done before. Leaders relish the opportunity to experiment, and they encourage others to be innovative. They tolerate errors and establish a framework of forgiveness, provided something is learned and gained from the experience. In so doing, they reduce the stress of learning from mistakes and create psychological hardiness for themselves and others.

Research has demonstrated that effective leaders have a hardy attitude that allows them to take change, chaos, stress, and even failure in stride (Kotter, 1996; Kouzes & Posner, 2007; Scott & Jaffe, 2004). They possess a mind-set that is stimulated by ongoing learning, improvement, and adventure. Leaders with this mind-set view a challenge as an opportunity to learn, rather than something to ignore or avoid.

"Being a risk-taker is not for the faint of heart."

Leaders who embrace change and take risks experience less stress and have a strong sense of control over their response, an unwavering belief they are doing something worthwhile, and a desire to learn from both positive and negative experiences. They also help their colleagues deal more effectively with risk by creating a climate that builds: 1) a sense of control, by choosing tasks that are challenging, yet within the person's competency level; 2) commitment, through more rewards than punishments; and 3) an attitude of challenge that encourages people to see change as opportunity (Kouzes & Posner, 2007).

Being a risk-taker is not for the faint of heart. It is perilous, involving uncertainty and loss. However, the benefits of learning—including increased sense of fulfillment and the reward of innovative experiences—can outweigh these factors.

 ## Confronting Racism*

It was a time of great violence and racial turbulence. A remarkable pair of citizen leaders in Detroit decided to challenge rampant racial inequity. One of them was a Catholic priest and the other a housewife. Their city was being torn apart by riots, racism, and hate, and most people were moving to the suburbs. The housewife, however, decided to leave her comfortable suburban home and move into the city with her family. The priest chose to stay at his inner-city parish. These individuals lost many friends along the way. Even family members ridiculed them and refused to visit, but the priest and the housewife wanted to help solve problems of inequity. Their decisions clearly reflected their values.

These two people became citizen activists. A small group of supporters joined them in organizing and training more than 50 clergy to help them confront hate, fear, and racism. This group saw an opportunity with summer coming—they decided to throw a huge street party to abate the violence that usually occurred. The mayor, bishop, police department, and others in positions of power fought the idea. The city council president told them, "If you bring a crowd downtown, you'll blow the city away!"

But the two persisted and decided they had to take the risk. They organized hundreds of volunteers of every color and creed. After weeks of exhausting work, their dream of a carnival in the streets where blacks, whites, and browns had fun together, rather than fight, materialized. No major negative incident occurred. The event was so successful that it received strong support from city leaders in subsequent years (Matusak, 1997).

*Paraphrased from the book *Finding Your Voice: Learning to Lead ... Anywhere You Want to Make a Difference*, by Larraine R. Matusak, Published in 1997, Jossey-Bass, San Francisco.

Leading Change

Change is the past, present, and future landscape for leaders. Once the decision to change has been made, it is incumbent on the leader to guide the change process through diligent strategy and careful execution.

Preparation is of utmost importance. All too frequently, leaders make decisions and announce a change and then immediately want to get started. Succumbing to this urge inevitably results in chaos and misalignment of action with intended outcomes. Good leaders move through the transformation process with unflinching commitment to the new vision. For example, they hold open forums to discuss issues and expectations. They are clear and focused in their vision and fulfillment of the change. They prepare and deliver a change plan and support its implementation.

"Leaders continually communicate the difference the change will bring to the vision and are undaunted by risk, reaction, and old rules."

Leaders recognize three assumptions about response to change, in addition to the emotional aspect. They know that group change requires individual change, and individual change helps others identify and examine their own capacity to change.

Each person has to figure out what the change means for them, their values, and their beliefs, and if they can function within the change. Leaders do this self-examination themselves and then model the way for others.

Leaders also know that no change can occur without keeping the destination in sight. They continually communicate the difference the change will bring to the vision and are undaunted by risk, reaction, and old rules. They are champions of change, and they enable others to embrace change.

Leaders recognize that the bigger and more drastic the change, and the larger the number of people who are involved in it, the more difficult it is to effect the change. Hence, they focus attention on the emotional response, carefully prepare a strategy, and monitor the implementation of a change.

Kotter (1996) defines an eight-stage process of creating major change, many of which have been discussed. As a recap, this process includes the following:

1. **Establishing a sense of urgency.** Leaders are well-prepared with data and trends that necessitate the need for change. They also work with experts to identify and discuss potential crises or opportunities. For example, a cardiac care nurse will understand therapy trends and outcomes before requesting implementation. Or, an emergency department nurse manager will plan for an influx of patients in the event of a natural disaster. Leaders convey the need to act now, based on sound information, rather than waiting for the disaster to occur or for patient mortality to rise, because a specific therapy has not been implemented.

2. **Creating a change team.** Leaders put together a cohort of people who have the authority to implement change. These change champions share the vision with the leader, as well as help set the agenda and prioritize actions to initiate and sustain the change. Motivated by the new vision, these individuals help disengage people from the past and get them hooked on the future.

3. **Keeping the vision alive.** Leaders not only create the vision, they also develop strategies for achieving it. For example, if the new vision is a more efficient transfer of information during nurse reporting, the leader might develop a strategy to do this electronically through a central portal that collects information charted at the bedside. This

potentially saves nurses time and effort. In leading change, the leader's ability to relate the activity to the vision is critical.

4. **Communicating the change vision.** Leaders use every possible vehicle to communicate the change vision and solicit change champions to join them. For example, leaders may develop posters for the workplace that show the new vision, send e-mail updates on progress, or place messages in the break room or newsletter. They help people become more comfortable with change by continually relating what is happening to the vision. The mind-set begins to shift to the new way of doing, thinking, and behaving.

5. **Enabling broad-based action.** Leaders change systems and practices that undermine the change vision. They set up experiments and make it safe for others to experiment. They enlist their change champions to help rid the environment of obstacles and encourage risk-taking and innovation. Leaders start with small steps toward the vision and give people choices.

   For example, a company decided to go with a central database for storage and access to all company data. No longer would people develop and keep their own databases; they would all be centralized and integrated. To implement this change, an experiment might first be set up in the finance department, where people could view accounts paid and invoices sent and received. The data would provide valuable information about what the customer purchased, paid for, or returned. An employee helping a customer could get a sense of the customer's preferences and could steer him or her in the direction of a similar satisfactory product.

6. **Generating short-term wins.** Leaders are careful to take incremental steps during the change process. People need to see that the change is working. It is, therefore, important that leaders immediately recognize wins—publicly and visibly. Leaders can also steer actions toward creating these wins.

   As an example, a school nurse was working to reduce childhood obesity in junior-high students. She identified and garnered the support of a core group of students. She worked with them on diet, nutrition, and exercise. First, she encouraged them to walk 15 minutes a day. When all students accomplished that, they celebrated their 100 percent exercise win. Next, the nurse encouraged them to substitute fruit for cookies in their lunch. When all the students achieved that goal, they celebrated. She incrementally guided them by developing healthy habits, rather than by setting up weight-loss expectations and diet and lifestyle changes at the same time.

7. **Consolidating more change and creating additional change opportunities.** Not everything will work and progress smoothly in a change process. That is why leaders admit and learn from mistakes. They do pre- and postmortems on projects, and make adaptations to fit the vision. Leaders get rid of systems, structures, and policies that don't fit with the new vision. They employ and leverage people who can implement the change vision and invigorate those around them.

For example, a clinical nurse specialist implemented a new protocol for diabetes management meant to reduce the incidence of high blood sugars. A few weeks after implementation, she discovered that the hyperglycemia incidence was increasing rather than decreasing. In doing a postmortem with her team, she discovered the barrier was a timing issue in both the pharmacy and hospital unit practices. While her experiment failed, her postmortem uncovered the problem, allowing her to work through a solution with the nurses and pharmacists.

8. **Anchoring new ways in the culture.** Sustaining a change is just as important as initiating it. Leaders integrate the change into the culture by pointing out the connection between new behaviors and organizational success. They demonstrate the value of the change by integrating development and reward systems into performance measures. They also pay attention to the morale and emotional tone of their followers.

One nurse manager, for example, pointed out to her staff how much more timely the change of shift report was after implementing an electronic medical record system. She also noted how medication errors and incidence reports had decreased, because caregivers had ready access to information, care plans, and precautions. She further noted and publicly recognized the change champions on the unit who had worked with her during the transition, rewarding them with gift certificates. Her approach was to establish positive outcomes because of the change and communicate its value to the vision of safe, high-quality care for patients.

Change is not all pain—it can actually be an exciting phenomenon. While change may be time-consuming and complicated, leaders consider periods of change to be some of the most challenging, growth-producing, exciting times of their careers.

Readiness and Reflection

Change happens in our personal, professional, and organizational lives. The following assessments allow you to check your personal and professional change readiness, your hardiness for change, and organizational readiness for change. Change can be sudden, unsettling, or welcome. It can be the result of factors in our personal or work worlds.

1. Change checklist: Check any changes listed below that you have gone through in the past year.*

   _____ I changed to a new type of work.

   _____ I changed work hours or conditions.

   _____ I increased or decreased work responsibilities.

   _____ I retired.

   _____ I was fired or laid off.

   _____ I took work-related courses.

   _____ I experienced trouble with co-workers.

   _____ The organization was reorganized.

   _____ Leadership changed in the organization.

   _____ New technology was introduced.

   _____ I experienced illness or injury.

   _____ I experienced a change in eating habits.

   _____ I experienced a change in sleeping habits.

   _____ I made a major purchase or acquired a mortgage.

   _____ I experienced a business reversal or financial loss.

   _____ I had a change in personal finances, good or bad.

   _____ I had a change in residence.

   _____ I experienced a change in the health of a family member.

   _____ I experienced other household change.

_____ I suffered the death of a spouse, family member, or friend.

_____ I got married or divorced.

_____ I welcomed a new family member.

_____ I had in-law problems.

_____ I separated or reconciled with my spouse.

_____ My spouse started or stopped working outside the home.

_____ I realized a major personal achievement.

_____ I made a major decision regarding the future.

_____ I started or stopped attending college.

_____ I experienced a change in religious beliefs.

_____ I had legal difficulties.

_____ I changed social activities or groups.

_____ I experienced theft or damage to personal property.

_____ I had an accident.

_____ I developed a new close personal relationship.

_____ I had a falling out in a close personal relationship.

Count up your total number of changes.

1-11: You are having an easy year.

12-21: Your year has been challenging.

22-29: You may need someone to help you through change.

30+: You are experiencing way too much change. Slow down!

*Adapted from Scott, C.D., & Jaffe, D. (2004). *Managing personal change.* Menlo Park, CA: Crisp Publications.

2. Personal Hardiness for Change: Of the following, check those that are true for you.

Commitment:

_____ I like what I am doing and who I am working for.

_____ I am eager to start the day's work.

_____ I have a sense of meaning and purpose.

_____ I feel that what I do is making a difference.

/

Challenge:

_____ I get excited and energized by new projects.

_____ I seek new opportunities as an important part of my life.

_____ I take on projects that stretch my ability.

Control:

_____ I spend my time on things I can do something about rather than what I can't control.

_____ At work, trying my best is the most effective approach when demands are high.

_____ I look for new ways to get things done.

Connection:

_____ I seek out other people when I need help or have a problem or difficulty.

_____ I feel that I give as much as I get from other people.

_____ I try to find out as much as I can from people around me.

If you checked fewer than two in any section, you need to work on your hardiness.

*Adapted from Scott, C.D., & Jaffe, D. (2004). *Managing personal change.* Menlo Park, CA: Crisp Publications.

3. Organizational Change Readiness. This tool will be useful for the leader when making plans with the change team. Rate each item below with a 1 (this is a problem area) to 5 (we are excellent at this).

_____ Change support is apparent at the highest level of the organization.

_____ There is a strong sense of urgency for this change.

_____ The organization has a culture that emphasizes continual improvement.

_____ We have a good track record at handling change.

_____ People understand how the change will help realize the values and vision of the organization.

_____ The change has clear objectives that are consistently communicated.

_____ The necessary resources can be mobilized.

_____ The change connects to other initiatives.

_____ People share information and cooperate with one another in their work.

_____ People can handle more change.

_____ The organization supports experiments and risk-taking to implement this change.

_____ People believe the change will benefit them.

_____ People like working in the organization and have a high level of responsibility.

_____ Mistakes are tolerated by the organization.

_____ Decisions are made quickly and communicated in a participatory style.

_____ Previous major changes have been successful.

_____ The higher the score, the more ready the organization is to take on change.

Adapted from Maurer, R. (1996). *Beyond the wall of resistance.* Austin, TX: Bard Press; and Abaris Consulting. (2001). *Organizational change readiness.* London, Ontario, Canada: Author.

4. Personal Risk Assessment. Read each of the descriptions below and assess the percentage of time this description applies to you. Rate each item below with a 1 if you feel this way most of the time. Rate each item with a 2 if you do NOT feel or behave this way most of the time.*

_____ Taking management risks makes good sense only if there are no acceptable alternatives.

_____ I generally prefer stimulation over serenity.

_____ I have confidence in my ability to recover from my mistakes, no matter how big.

_____ I would promote someone with unlimited potential, but limited experience, to a key position over someone with limited potential, but more experience.

_____ Anything worth doing is worth doing less than perfectly.

_____ I believe opportunity knocks only once.

_____ It is better to ask for permission than to beg for forgiveness.

_____ Success in management is as much a matter of luck as ability.

_____ Given a choice, I would choose a $3,000 annual raise over a $10,000 bonus that I had a one-in-three chance of receiving.

_____ I can handle big losses and disappointments with little difficulty.

_____ If forced to choose, I would choose safety over achievement.

_____ Failure is the long way to management success.

_____ I tolerate ambiguity and unpredictability well.

_____ I would rather feel intense disappointment than intense regret.

_____ When making a decision with uncertain consequences, potential losses are my greatest concern.

If you assigned a rating of 1 to items 2, 3, 4, 5, 10, or 13, give yourself one point for each.

If you assigned a rating of 2 to items 1, 6, 7, 8, 9, 11, 12, or 15, give yourself one point for each.

Calculate your total. A score of 11 or higher indicates strong pro-risk attitudes, 6-10 indicates a moderate pro-risk attitude, and 5 or below indicates a weak pro-risk attitude.

*Adapted from Calvert, G. (1993). *Highwire management.* San Francisco, CA: Jossey-Bass.

5. Ask your change team to complete one or more of these assessments. Discuss with them how the assessment relates to the success of your change initiative.

6. As the leader of a change initiative, planning is of utmost importance to success. Before communicating the change to others, spend time thinking and strategizing about the following:

   - How was the initiative selected, and how does it fit into the organization's overall objective?

   - Have I clearly defined the initiative, the need for it, and the benefits?

   - What are the major objectives and milestones?

   - How will the goals for the initiative be determined?

   - What team members, resources, and support will I need?

   - How will I select the team members?

   - What is my timeline? Is it realistic?

   - Who are the stakeholders, and how do I secure their buy-in?

   - How will I keep momentum going once the initiative is underway?

   - Do I need a mentor or sponsor to help the team, and me, stay on track?

7. Reflect on what you have learned from this chapter and your responses to the exercises. Write a paragraph about where you see yourself today as a change agent and risk-taker.

8. Develop two strategies to improve your skills for leading change and taking risk, and add them to your personal leadership development plan.

Chapter 12

Strategy Is Just Another Word for Work: Being Strategic

There was a time when strategic planning was the answer for whatever faced a leader or organization, but no more. Because change is not a one-time event, but a constant state for people and groups, successful leadership is built on the ability to sense and rapidly adjust to a changing environment.

Rather than diving in and creating strategic plans, true leaders engage in strategic learning, a process that gains focus from what is learned, aligns the learning with purpose, and designs action to meet the purpose in an adaptive mode. By living in this cycle of learning, focusing, aligning, and executing, leaders create responsive, proactive teams and organizations (Pietersen, 2002).

Mintzberg (1994), who has studied what really happens in strategic development, makes clear that much strategic planning comes to a dead end. His findings are startling. Ninety percent of the results projected in formal strategic plans of most companies never come to fruition—they simply fall by the wayside as unrealized strategy. Only 10 percent of companies' actions and results arise from the strategic plan.

"Strategy is basically about making choices."

So what are the sources of the other 90 percent? According to Mintzberg, the sources are emergent strategy or actions—reactions, decisions, choices, and initiatives taken in response to environmental pressure. This is the real strategy most companies take, frequently with little guidance from the overarching strategic plan. Rather than following the linear path of most strategic plans, these leaders, in determining action, cycle what they learn from the environment, focusing, aligning and executing action that complements the company's purpose.

Pietersen's (2002) explanation for this is quite simple: Strategy begins with divergent thinking, whereas planning is an exercise in convergent thinking. If leaders are to unleash the creativity and empowerment needed to achieve excellence, it is essential that they separate strategy from planning, and place strategy first.

The Strategist

"In a world of increasing complexity and uncertainty, leaders must help their organizations develop the ability to make sense of the changing environment."

Strategy is basically about making choices. As applied to organizational or team work, it is about how the group will succeed, based on the best deployment of scarce resources. Strategy is focusing on the things that yield success.

People who are strategic continually ask "what if" and shift through all sorts of information to find the best approach to an issue. They have a distinct way of thinking about the world at large that allows them to identify patterns. Being mindful of the patterns, they play out scenarios and alternatives, always asking, "What if this happens?" They are always looking around the corner for what is next and, in doing so, identify and evaluate potential obstacles. Guided by where the "what ifs" take them, they begin selecting the best actions to take, discarding options that will lead nowhere, cause confusion, or encounter impenetrable resistance (Buckingham & Clifton, 2001).

The Nurse Strategist

Dennis was an associate dean in charge of multiple nursing programs at a moderate size university. The school had recently received a strategic directive from the dean that enrollment across all programs would increase by 15 percent in the coming years. Dennis and his program heads had nine months to plan for this change.

Dennis knew this decision had been based on multiple factors: the need for more nurses in the community; an increased interest in the profession by individuals already holding degrees; and a university expectation of increased enrollment. He also recognized there was a faculty and clinical-site shortage, and competition for both was high in the geographic area. Dennis knew he had to first determine his faculty's capacity to meet this increased demand before embarking on a strategic solution to the directive.

As he met with his program heads about their needs, strengths, and goals, Dennis quickly realized there was little synchrony among them, and not a great deal of alignment with the school's mission to prepare knowledgeable, ethical, and safe practitioners for the workforce. He also realized there was a great deal of expertise and intellectual ability among the program heads that was untapped.

Recognizing these patterns of misalignment, nonsynchrony, and underutilized expertise, Dennis initiated a series of meetings with the program heads. During the first meeting, he asked them to evaluate their contribution to the school's mission and objectives. The second meeting focused on Dennis' assessment and observations, as well as gaps revealed by the group's self-evaluations, and ended with the heads identifying where their strengths could fill the gaps.

By the next meeting, Dennis had synthesized all this information. He mapped out a picture of what *could* be *if* people worked across programs, focused on their areas of expertise, and brought in partners from the community. Subsequent meetings were spent discussing challenges to their vision, devising different scenarios, and continually asking "what if."

For example, a challenge in using one facility as a clinical site was sidestepped by asking *what if* they used the community health center. Another issue was strategized by identifying two faculty members who had strong administration skills and asking *what if* they assumed primary responsibility for administrative details, while others assumed some of their teaching load.

After several months of strategic thinking with the heads and, eventually, faculty members who reported to them, Dennis was able to refocus the programs and faculty on purpose, realign them with mission, repurpose work to fit their strengths, reframe their responsibilities and contributions, and create a new synchrony across the group. His ability to see the big picture, think in patterns, and determine logical consequences of actions led to the strategic solution needed to address the dean's directive.

Strategist Skills

Leaders who are strategists have the ability to lead people in discovering the answers to these four questions:

1. What is the environment in which we must work and succeed?

2. What are three to five things we must do outstandingly well and keep on doing to succeed?

3. How will we measure success?

4. How will we align the organization and inspire people to achieve success?

Naturally, answers to these questions vary from organization to organization. It is the leader's responsibility to pose these powerful questions and ultimately to make sense of the data gleaned from them. The leader, above all others, must clearly understand and communicate the environment, mission, success needed, and how to reach success.

To reach this level of clarity and purposeful action, leaders exhibit and employ several distinct competencies: insight, focus, alignment, execution, and renewal (Pietersen, 2002). Their ability to deploy these skills helps their groups and organizations succeed.

- **Insight**: In a world of increasing complexity and uncertainty, leaders must help their organizations develop the ability to make sense of the changing environment. Superior insight of leaders produces a winning edge for their organizations. For example, one nurse director observed an increasing number of Hispanic patients in the population her health care system served. She secured funds for her staff nurses to learn Spanish, so they could more effectively communicate with their patients. This director made sense of a changing landscape of patients in her health care system.

- **Focus**: Zeroing in on the right thing to do with the insight gained is an additional strength of leaders in an era of change. For example, a nurse entrepreneur recognized the importance of nurses having current knowledge and evidence at the bedside. In cooperation with a major technology company, the entrepreneur developed the ability to capture this information in electronic medical records used at the patient's bedside. The nurse focused on finding a practical, efficient way to assist nurses in providing evidence-based care.

- **Alignment**: Effective leaders have the ability to align every aspect of their team project or organization behind the strategic focus. While this is a monumental challenge, the strategy will not succeed without this alignment. The story of Dennis, told earlier in this chapter, illustrates this concept.

- **Execution**: Implementing the strategy in a timely manner is also key to success. Speed in carrying out a strategy improves the ability of the leader and organization to take advantage of the next environmental shift and expands the ability to stay in front of changes. For, example, a prominent nursing organization first went online in 1993, before the World Wide Web was readily accessible and before other companies had strategized about the Web. When the Internet became available to

> *"Effective leaders have the ability to align every aspect of their team project or organization behind the strategic focus."*

all, the organization was already positioned to move most of its services to an electronic format for those members who opted for that delivery method, as well as open its doors wider to a global community network.

- **Renewal**: Strategic leaders know that, to maintain a winning edge, they must have the ability to do these things over and over. They create an ongoing cycle of learning, focusing, aligning, and succeeding.

For example, consider the hospital that seeks and gains approval as a Magnet facility. The chief nursing executive realizes this is not a one-time change, but a state of excellence that requires continual action with regard to each of the forces of Magnetism. The executive will build a team to assess and glean data from the hospital industry. She will focus on the prominent health and workforce issues influencing the safety and quality of care in her institution. She will align them with the hospital's health care and economic goals and implement new strategies that contribute to the success of the hospital and showcase nursing's contribution.

The Strategist's Strategies

When leaders engage these skills and ask powerful questions, they are being intentionally strategic. Rather than allowing change and circumstances to dictate a course of action, strategic leaders think and act in an adaptable, nimble way to best serve those they lead and represent. Once learning, focus, and alignment are clear, strategic leaders consider six elements when making decisions.

1. **Define outcomes *before* identifying tasks.** Strategic leaders approach work by asking, "What will be different as a result of our work?" The emphasis is on *what*, not *how*.

   We have all participated in strategic planning meetings and been a part of the tactical onslaught. It is a natural inclination to go straight to the tactics, or how something gets done, rather than focusing on the "something" the group wishes to accomplish. For example, an issue for a hospital unit might be the rising incidence of pressure ulcers. Rather than leading off the discussion with "We need to do this or add this or change these," strategists start the discussion by asking, "What will be different as a result of our work?"

"Rather than allowing change and circumstances to dictate a course of action, strategic leaders think and act in an adaptable, nimble way to best serve those they lead and represent."

This approach leads to a focus on desired outcome, perhaps reduction of pressure ulcers by 20 percent in eight months, rather than identifying pieces in the process. There are many ways to achieve an outcome—this is where individual creativity and innovation come into play. But there is only one focus, and that is on what is to be achieved.

2. **Plan with intention, rather than work by rationale.** Leaders know that results can be achieved through many tasks and activities. It is easy to retrofit actions to goals. This is called working by rationale. Because this approach is not strategically focused on what will be different, many of the tasks do not align with goals or values and thus require additional work to ensure congruence.

   For example, a group of staff nurses has a desired outcome of implementing evidence-based practice in a neonatal unit to provide state-of-the-science care. A lunchtime journal club has been established to help meet this goal. While the activity is laudable and helpful, it's important to ask, "How does this journal club meet the outcome of actually providing evidence-based care?"

   If, on the other hand, planning with intention has occurred, the lunch bunch might use the knowledge gained from the journal club to develop care plans or protocols for infants based on evidence, guidelines, expertise, and family preferences. Rather than just reading or discussing information, this approach puts knowledge about the best available evidence into action.

3. **Take into account the external environment.** Every organization or unit is part of something larger. Leaders must understand the big picture and the role each individual plays. They do this by understanding the context—what is happening around them—and reflecting the context in goals they set and actions they take. How leaders communicate and what they communicate are also important.

The external environment can influence, shape, and impact the work at hand. Paying close attention to the environment enhances the leader's ability to be successful over time. For example, that neonatal unit is part of a pediatrics department that aspires to quality, family-friendly care. The department is part of a health care system that focuses on safe, cost-effective care. To gain support of evidence-based care plans, the nurses would need to demonstrate and communicate all these factors. The mission and values of the environments would need to intentionally relate to their desired outcome, as expressed by this statement: Evidence-based nursing care achieves safety, contains costs, and provides quality, family-centered care.

4. **Use facts, knowledge, and expertise.** Having good ideas, a plan, or even stated outcomes is not enough anymore. Leaders and their teams must use facts, knowledge, and expertise to assess their situation, inform a course of action, and engage others in the collective work.

> *"Leaders work in the present with an eye to the future, rather than working in the present to correct the past."*

Often, leaders assess facts and then use their own knowledge and expertise, and that of others, to do the work. As actions and outcomes are being considered, leaders ask early and often, "What do I know or not know about this situation or issue?" They frequently seek advice and perspective from others. This intelligence is then used for planning. For example, the nurses in the neonatal unit who wish to implement evidence-based practices need to determine the interest of their supervisor, nurse co-workers, and perhaps the head of neonatology in implementing these practices. Securing the commitment and expertise of these key individuals will expedite action toward the desired outcome.

5. **Incorporate a barometer of the future.** Being intentionally strategic takes more than solving the issue of the day. It requires asking, "How will this be influenced by the future?" Leaders work in the present with an eye to the future, rather than working in the present to correct the past. For the neonatal unit nurses who want to provide evidence-based practice, this means knowing about the

uptake of these practices. They need to answer questions such as: Is this a fad? Do others in the department see this as a sustainable future? Does the organization value this practice? Thinking about the future provides continuity and ensures sustainability of the work.

6. **Assess resources.** None of the leader's strategic, knowledgeable, futuristic planning will accomplish the desired outcomes without resources. These resources may be people, money, time, or all three.

Leaders understand that it is incredibly important to identify and develop their resources. Resource development calls for creativity and innovation. It requires the leader to be clear about what is needed and where the most appropriate place is to secure it. Resource management becomes a major skill for leaders to deploy.

For example, the neonatal nurses would secure support from their supervisor and co-workers. They would consider any resource material costs associated with development of the protocols and release time to perform the research or teach staff members who are implementing the protocols. They would assume leadership for selling their desired outcome and securing the resources to make it a reality.

"Leaders understand that it is incredibly important to identify and develop their resources."

Leaders understand the value of strategy and place it in the context of learning. They seek to find relevant focus and alignment in what they learn from others, the environment, and the future. In some ways, leaders allow actions to reveal themselves through this deliberate, intentional thinking. Then, leaders make decisions about what actions would maximize their limited resources, while building processes that promote renewal of this cycle.

Readiness and Reflection

1. Assess your strategic quotient by answering "yes" or "no" to the following questions. I consistently:

   _____ Engage myself and my team in divergent thinking.

   _____ Look at what is happening in my professional and work environment before making decisions.

   _____ Focus on the right thing to do that will make a difference, versus doing the right thing.

   _____ Identify priority areas for action.

   _____ Define anticipated outcomes before performing tasks.

   _____ Focus on what will be different as a result of my actions.

   _____ Use facts and information in decision-making, rather than follow my instinct alone.

   _____ Consider the sustainability of actions I plan and implement.

   _____ Implement actions in a timely manner.

   _____ Learn from the decisions I make and actions I take.

   _____ Refocus direction and action if I am off-track.

   _____ Align what I do with the goals of the team or organization.

   _____ Enable my team to get behind the strategic focus.

   _____ Know where to tap into resources to realize my goals.

   _____ Manage and cultivate resources well.

   Add up your "yes" responses. If you have 1-5, your strategic ability has a good start. Now is the time to select skills and work with a mentor to further develop them. If you have 6-11, you are using a good mix of strategic skills and would benefit from further development of skills you responded "no" to. If you have 12-16 "yes" responses, your strategic abilities are well-grounded and used. Continue to hone your skills.

2. With your team, engage in a strategic-thinking exercise on a key issue affecting your success in the workplace, using the six strategist strategies.

3. Consider an action or initiative that did not go as well as you anticipated. What did you learn from this experience? What would you do differently now?

4. Identify a person who you believe exhibits and makes use of strategist skills. Have a conversation with that person about a successful initiative that he or she undertook. Discuss the thinking that went into planning and implementing the project.

5. Reflect on what you have learned in this chapter and from the exercises. Write one paragraph on where you see yourself today as a strategist.

6. Develop two strategies you can take to enhance your strategic leadership skills, and add them to your personal leadership development plan.

Part III

Go Lead!

Leadership is first and foremost about who a person is and what he or she stands for. The truest level of leadership occurs when the person's beliefs and principles are visible and evident in strategy and action. No amount of self discovery, talent mining, development, or leadership competency will make a difference for others unless it is articulated into action.

Moving the leadership *self* onto the leadership stage can be a risky proposition. Not only do leaders have to continually develop their own selves, they must also cultivate their followers, their organizations, and their environments. The dynamic, complex process of leadership requires the leader to be ever ready to lead intentionally, creatively, and with deliberateness in uncertain times.

Leading tests not only leaders' abilities and the state of their leadership, it also challenges the leader to take risks while bringing others along toward the desired result. The risk of leadership is a bit like walking into a dark cave with only a pen light. Unable to see clearly to the end of the cave, the leader calls to the followers to join him or her in the darkness. Trusting in themselves and their followers, leaders willingly take this risk.

Leadership is not easy. In fact, it can be downright harrowing. Unless the leader takes that first step and acts with conviction, nothing great will occur. At some point in time, all leaders must simply *go lead!*

Chapter 13

Arts and Crafts in the Conference Room: Being Creative, Innovative, and Resourceful

Leaders intuitively know that creativity and innovation are vital in this age of continual change and challenges. As Porter-O'Grady (2002) observes: "Change is. People don't make change. They give it form and link it to all elements that will either constrain or facilitate it" (p. 336).

Change causes disequilibrium in people, resulting in fluctuations, disturbance, and imbalances. It challenges the very being and meaning of what is in a person's or an organization's world. Reaction to change creates chaos. Leaders know, however, that this time of chaos is a primary source of creativity and innovation.

Creativity and innovation co-exist, but are not the same. Creativity is the generation of new ideas, thoughts, or concepts. These notions are original and appropriate, involving the simple act of generating something new and relevant. Innovation, on the other hand, is the process of applying creativity in a specific context. In an organizational context, for example, innovation generally refers to conversion of creative ideas into novel, useful, and viable practices or services.

Innovation begins with creativity. Leaders recognize that creativity is the first step—the starting point—for innovation. Unless something is done with an idea, it remains just that, a thought. Leaders understand the importance of the marriage of creativity and innovation to the success of groups, and they promote this union to prevent obsolescence, increase productivity, and enhance the meaning and reward of work.

The Spirit of Creativity

Creativity is not some mystical power bestowed on a chosen few. We all have it—just take a look at any group of children and witness their wonder, curiosity, and boldness. But somewhere along life's journey, these traits are shaped, stopped, and maybe even warped, making it difficult for adults to let what they naturally have arise and take form.

Leaders reignite their creativity, however, through self-awareness and developed discipline. Knowing the importance of creativity to the difference they wish to make in their organization and the world, leaders seek out opportunities to get in touch with and express their creative selves, both in their personal lives and work situations.

"Creativity is not some mystical power bestowed on a chosen few. We all have it— just take a look at any group of children and witness their wonder, curiosity, and boldness."

For example, some individuals take time every day to let their thoughts flow freely, often writing down these thoughts and ideas as they form. Other people exercise reflective time every day, reviewing what happened and what could have been done differently. New ideas often arise from these moments of reflection. Still others engage in workshops and seminars on building personal creativity. In other words, leaders take time to look for opportunities to identify and develop expressions of their creativity. They know they have to tap their own creativeness before they can expect their followers to discover and explore theirs.

The creative spirit allows leaders to engage in divergent, open-ended thinking that has no single right answer, as opposed to convergent thinking that pursues one correct answer. Because creative leaders are open to different thought, they are adaptable, flexible, and tolerant of ambiguity. Their take on a challenge is that there is no one correct way to address it, but rather a new way. They search for an original response to a challenge and, in doing so, question the status quo. Creative leaders go outside the realm of rules, rituals, and routine, departing from existing norms to make sense of the issue. They seek autonomy of thought away from the constraints of organizational patterns and structure.

 ## The Power of Brainstorming

In her job as a nurse practitioner in a primary-care setting, Diane was feeling bored and stifled by the mechanical repetitiveness of her job. Every day, it was one patient after another, all with similar complaints or coming for routine annual examinations. It was the same lab tests, same prescriptions, and same prevention education. The system and protocols were set up that way, and no one challenged the administration to do things differently.

Diane felt she and her colleagues were prepared and had the knowledge to do much more, such as manage patients with chronic illnesses, do post-surgery rounds on patients in the hospital and immediately upon discharge, or conduct home visits for homebound patients. These were responsibilities she and her co-workers had discussed many times over lunch breaks and outside clinic hours. She began thinking about the situation.

Every day, riding to and from work on the subway, she would think, just think. Then she began to write her thoughts down, asking "what if" we did this or that. This went on for several weeks and, while she did not have her answer, she felt she was coming up with some great ideas. But she needed more information and data about practice models for nurse practitioners in similar settings.

At this point, Diane shared with two of her nurse practitioner colleagues what she had been doing. Immediately, the three started brainstorming and sharing some of their thoughts. All of them had been trying to discover expression for their creative thoughts but, fearful of reprimand and being cast as a troublemaker, had kept them to themselves. Now they had unity of purpose and a shared dream that would make them feel more fulfilled and be more productive. They just didn't quite have the solution figured out yet.

For the next several weeks, the three talked incessantly about the "what ifs," until they reached what they thought was the end of their exploration. But, several days later, as Diane was riding home and jotting thoughts in her journal, a solution hit her like a bolt of lightning. She hurriedly wrote her thoughts down and called her comrades as soon as she got home. Her proposal was that the three of them embark on a pilot project for 6 months, with each taking responsibility for one of the three areas they wished to expand into. One would follow up with post-surgical patients two mornings a week; one would increase her case load of diabetic patients and manage them, as this was a chronic condition prevalent in their patient population; and the third would make home visits 1 day a week to homebound patients.

During the 6-month trial period, all three agreed to shorten visit times for routine exams to 20 minutes, to accommodate the patient load left uncovered by their shift in schedules. The nurse practitioners' appointments would all be covered. All three were energized by the proposal, which they spent several weeks developing before taking it to the administration.

Their "sell" job was not an easy one. They were bucking the system and creating uncertainty in many areas, including access of patients to their provider, cost of the pilot program, and changes in protocol, to name a few. But they were persistent, well-prepared with facts and knowledge and, most of all, convincing in their claim that this different, new idea would be successful. The pilot was approved.

In the end, two of the three shifts in responsibility were successful. The home visits were not as productive as hoped. The center adopted the changes permanently and even expanded the chronic-illness management part of the program to include patients with other dominant health issues. Other practitioners accepted differing responsibilities when offered the opportunity, and the three were recognized at an annual dinner for their contribution. Creativity brought the new practices into being, and innovation breathed life into the ideas.

Creativity Traits in Leaders

Leaders express creativity in ways as diverse as they are, but dominant characteristics do surface repeatedly in the literature (Klemm, 2001; Kouzes and Posner, 2007). These traits allow leaders to forge new pathways and provide a comprehensive context for their work. Creative leaders are:

- great at generating ideas,
- always looking to experiment with good ideas,
- quick to pose open-ended questions,
- prepared and have a desire to be creative,
- firm believers in originality in thought and action,
- smart and bright, with a positive self-image, but not geniuses,
- expressive, and sensitive to their surroundings and the people in them,
- well-informed and loathe to make snap decisions,
- nonconformists, requiring less social approval than most,
- independent and demonstrate sound judgment,
- innately able to understand and solve problems,
- able to manage consequences, and
- dreamers with strong imaginations, yet able to keep things in perspective.

Creativity can be expressed in a multitude of ways: drawings, stories, scenarios, humor, role-playing, and so forth. Determining *how* to express creativity is up to the individual. Not only are leaders creative, they also encourage those around them to be creative.

Leaders form the work environment that enables creativity. They treat every job as an adventure and create meaningful challenges for those around them. Leaders are not threatened by out-of-the-box thinking and are quick to recognize and use good ideas, qualities that make others feel secure.

"Leaders stimulate people to be creative. They visibly show their enthusiasm and determination to make something different happen."

Creativity in Nursing Practice

Sally, a staff nurse on a maternity unit, regarded every patient who came in as a new experience. She took time to get to know them and their families. Knowing that labor and delivery are stressful, both physically and emotionally, she gave her patients a lot of latitude in doing what made them feel comfortable. In some ways, she let the patient and family members run the show, while she monitored their safety and well-being.

She took special interest in fathers who were befuddled, scared, and confused. She allayed a father's fears by having him with her as she monitored the patient, explaining what she was doing and why. Sally also used humor with patients and their families to diffuse tension and sometimes discomfort.

Leaders also expect creativity in others—if people know they are expected to be creative, they work harder at it. When their creativity progresses to the innovation stage, they feel ownership and pride, working even harder to see their ideas come to fruition.

To reach a better way, leaders provide a climate and culture for discussion and disagreement. They give themselves and their team time to think and create.

 ## Shopping for ideas

Steve is a nurse manager in the operating room. He has regular weekly meetings with staff nurses, which he calls "shopping for ideas." During this time, he expects people to bring their brightest ideas for improving efficiency and productivity in the operating room. Since these meetings began more than a year ago, the team has implemented new staffing schedules, different prep practices, and rotation of responsibilities. As a result, staff members are enjoying their work more and feel a deeper commitment to the team.

Leaders stimulate people to be creative. They visibly show their enthusiasm and determination to make something different happen. They challenge others by assigning work that matches strengths and talents. They provide hospitable space and formal means for brainstorming and developing ideas. In addition, they know how to get the right people together to generate ideas, and they engage people of diverse backgrounds and ages. They create analysis teams to examine issues and periodically refresh their teams with new people who can bring different ideas and solutions.

 ## Brain Parties

Betty was a nursing professor who was quite passionate about leadership education for nurses. In her paid university position and her volunteer professional positions, she worked to improve leadership education of nurses.

She regularly held what she called "brain parties," inviting no more than 10 people to a location outside the workplace. For a meeting on leadership experience for senior baccalaureate students, she invited three students who had leadership potential, two clinical nurse managers who were skilled leaders in patient care, a nurse entrepreneur friend, and two of her fellow faculty members. The question to be addressed was: What type of experience would prepare beginning nurses to exercise leadership in the patient care setting?

The meeting was held in Betty's backyard, as it was a beautiful spring day, and the environment was peaceful, relaxed, and conducive to thinking. In addition to many other ideas, the meeting produced one especially good idea that all felt would create an awesome experience for learning about leadership. Students would work in groups of five, and each group would identify a key health issue in the care settings where the nurse managers worked. Under faculty supervision, the students would develop a new approach for this issue and, with the nurse managers' guidance, implement the idea. Throughout the process, students would write about their experience in leadership development in a journal.

Another example of how Betty stimulated creativity was her idea about forming a leadership academy that was offered through her professional organization. She realized that many nurses did not receive true leadership content during their educational experiences, yet were placed in leadership roles. This time, Betty brought together a multidisciplinary group to address the question: What leadership contribution does nursing make to the health of people? She felt that analyzing and understanding the disparity between what is perceived and what is lived out would provide direction in how to fill the gaps.

Economists, health administrators, futurists, policy-makers, payers, physicians, and nurses comprised the group. After 2 days of data analysis, conversation, and debate, the group delivered a response to the question posed, plus a set of recommendations for the organization to consider. In both instances, Betty brought a diverse, but appropriate, mix of people together, provided an amicable environment for them to think and create, and enlisted their expertise to solve issues.

Leaders make things happen, and have a knack for finding and unleashing the people who are most involved and immersed in a particular issue. Not surprisingly, those who know a great deal about the situation or issue tend to come up with the best ideas, so leaders encourage them. They also create an open approach to finding opportunities and, to gain a different perspective, invite others not directly related to the issue.

Once ideas start to flow and take form, leaders communicate and extol creativity, breaking down barriers to receptivity. Then, leaders give their creative teams autonomy to move forward, with each member knowing that to be successful, he or she is responsible to the team, and the team knowing that it is responsible to the organization.

Creativity in Crisis

Patricia owned a successful nurse staffing business that served client organizations across the northeast United States. When disaster struck in the form of a hurricane, her offices were wiped out, and her home was in jeopardy of flooding. Despite these seemingly insurmountable problems, Patricia knew she somehow had to keep the business and assignments running. Local hospitals depended on her to supply them with nurses, and she had a primary concern for her nurses' welfare as well.

She pulled together her senior management team, which also was dealing with issues, and developed a plan for recovery of essential services in 3 days and full recovery within 2 weeks. This was creativity under crisis. Her team seized the initiative—using a business recovery service, partnering with suppliers and clients, and forming alliances with competitors.

The team did the majority of the work—calling, negotiating, and meeting with clients and partners—while Patricia found opportunities and options for keeping the business running. In the end, she was able to meet her hospital clients' needs and keep nurses working who wanted and were able to work, while also helping her family and team members' families relocate and settle.

One of the most important things leaders do to ignite creativity is to build a system for rewarding those who are creative. People need to know that their ideas are valued and useful, so leaders allow others to participate in formulating policies and making decisions. Leaders eliminate conformity and the fear of failure and reprimand for bright ideas. They recognize error and, by paving the way to learn from mistakes, generate the next wave of ideas.

A simple, yet effective, example of this is the employee suggestion box. The leader reviews suggestions, selecting the best ones for development. The author of the idea leads the team in that development. The

"Leaders make things happen, and have a knack for finding and unleashing the people who are most involved and immersed in a particular issue."

leader, however, recognizes all ideas individually and publicly. When a decision or policy has to be made, the team relies on the developers and implementers to illuminate them with their best thinking.

Some leaders initiate annual creativity awards for ideas that have made the most significant difference to the organization. Still others provide monetary incentives or added benefits to creative innovators. The notion is to change attitudes and provide positive outcomes that encourage creativity.

Innovation

Innovations don't just fall from the heavens. Developed from a creative idea, innovations intentionally bring into existence something new that can be sustained. Innovations also bring value and relevance to their developers and users. Innovation breathes life and form into the creative notion.

Innovative processes are inherently uncertain and complex. It is far easier to come up with a bright idea than to develop it into fruition. Innovation causes people to search for new meaning in what and how they do something. It mandates examining and questioning the status quo, and the road from innovation to application is long and frequently hazardous. The primary reasons for this paradox—the excitement of coming up with something new versus the trepidation that accompanies the prospect of bringing it into existence—are linked to several factors.

"Innovations don't just fall from the heavens."

First is the variability of people's response to the innovation. The consequences to the organization's social, economic, and cultural structure must be considered. Responses to innovation may be hard to predict. In times of innovation and transformation, leaders call forth all of their competencies to achieve success.

Second, uncertainty is fed by limited knowledge. Whatever it is, the innovation is new and, hence, has little in the way of evidence, measurement, or observation to indicate its potential for success. Needless to say, this makes people uneasy. This is when the leader calls on his or her shared-vision, risk-taking, and strategic-planning abilities to help people find significance in the innovation. A leader must sell the idea effectively and keep those to whom they are accountable well-informed.

Third, limited resources for developing an innovation often contribute to both its uncertainty and complexity. Lack of adequate human and fiscal resources is the most common reason an innovation fails, coupled with nonbelief in its benefit. These factors require the leader to be creative about financing options, as well as staffing options. Development and implementation processes must be well-planned, demonstrating that constraints can be overcome. This is why leaders build a team of change champions, make the innovation a priority for everyone in the organization, are strategic and patient, and celebrate small wins along the way (Porter-O'Grady & Malloch, 2002).

Resourcefulness

Leaders are capable of dealing with difficult situations at a moment's notice. They find solutions and create ways to accomplish what needs to be done. Resourcefulness complements the leader's creativity, particularly as ideas become innovations.

Resources take many forms: expertise, time, money, people, equipment, information, and data. Leaders place a premium on sharing and stretching resources to accomplish what needs to be done. To do this, they encourage others to make a commitment to the common goal and promote the philosophy of "what is mine is ours" in resource allocation. Leaders establish a norm of reciprocity and encourage people to share information, listen to each other's ideas, exchange resources, and respond to each other's requests through positive interdependence (Kouzes & Posner, 2007). They expect high-level cooperation and collaboration.

People demonstrate resourcefulness through many behaviors. During Hurricane Katrina, who can forget how nurses and physicians devised portable equipment to protect their patients during evacuation? Or, there is the parent who helps a child build a science project out of leftover pieces of wood. Then there is the student who, running low on tuition money, finds a part-time job and low-interest loan. Every day, people are inventive and resourceful in their lives, demonstrating that the spirit of creativity is very much alive.

Leaders also demonstrate resourcefulness in many ways, but consistently pay attention to these six elements of resourcefulness:

- Leaders equally develop inner resources, such as values and beliefs, and outer resources, such as money and time.

- Leaders build a repository of knowledge and information that everyone can tap into to get the job done.

- Leaders surround themselves and the organization with an expert group of people with talents and skills the organization needs to meet its mission.

- Leaders delegate authority and power to individuals and groups to discern the issues and find solutions.

- Leaders forge relationships, partnerships, and alliances with those outside the organization who will work with them in the best interest of the organization.

- Leaders lay the groundwork for focused work by prioritizing, organizing, planning, and managing time.

Being resourceful is a value-added, complementary competency for leaders to develop. It facilitates quick-focused action and engages people across the organization.

The Innovation Process

The complexity of the basic innovation process encompasses the elements of uncertainty, but also requires leaders to consider the following:

- The uniqueness of the innovation: Is it really new and of value to the organization?

- The economic impact of the innovation: Will there be a return on resources invested by the organization?

- Consensus, or lack thereof, of stakeholders: Do those served need and value the innovation?

- The vision of the innovation and its alignment with the organization: What will this innovation do to serve the organization's mission?

- Barriers and risks to the innovation's success: What does a risk assessment tell about the social, cultural, economic, and technological response?

- Organizational fitness to undergo the innovation: Is the organization ready for transformational change?

- Time factor of development and implementation: What is the timeline, and are we able to deliver the innovation while the need is still great?

- Success measures: How will we know if the innovation is successful?

Answers to these questions frequently generate other questions specific to the innovation and organization. Leaders carefully guide people through the innovation quagmire, fueled by their belief, passion, and competency.

Leaders stimulate innovation and creativity in many ways. They ask people to come up with one new idea a day, or give permission to pick an organizational rule to break that won't cause harm. They encourage people to read about creativity and innovation, often passing along materials they have discovered. Most of all, they encourage people to think unbridled by constraints, to think wildly, and to think of many solutions, not just one.

"Leaders encourage people to think unbridled by constraints, to think wildly, and to think of many solutions, not just one."

 ## The Innovator

Anthony is a leader who firmly believes in innovation. He never met a challenge he didn't like or embrace with enthusiasm. He was the new dean in a small university system that was experiencing low licensure scores for its graduates. The decline in the pass rate had been steady for three years, leveling off for another two. The school's reputation was suffering, as was enrollment. Anthony knew all these challenges when he accepted the position, and felt he was the right person to bring something new to life for the school.

Anthony knew he had to engage everyone with an interest in the school: students, parents, faculty, donors, and administration. And he had to do it in spirited, new ways. He started with the faculty and students, then quickly progressed to the others. He challenged the traditional top down structure and stimulated others to try something new. Scheduling of clinical experiences was changed first, to cover the 24 hours that patients are in the hospital, requiring care. Doing this meant scheduling classes in a new way, so that students received all required theory content before or as they were having their clinical experiences.

Anthony then tackled the curriculum, capitalizing on the expertise of the department chairs for instructional decision-making. These people were the teacher-leaders, and they reshaped the curriculum to include more updated content and models. They got out of the mode of "We've always done it this way" and into the mode of "What can we do differently to teach our students?"

Lastly, Anthony formed a team to look at admission requirements and prerequisites so that students who were accepted were best prepared to take on the rigors of the new nursing curriculum. The team delivered rigorous admission criteria that were aligned with those of the university. It was implemented immediately.

In the first year, licensure exam pass rates went up, but not significantly. Patience, Anthony advised, reiterating all the reasons for it. Support across the campus and from other deans was not great at this point, and Anthony was advised not to challenge the top anymore, to get back in step with everyone else. There was only one solution for Anthony: He and his team had to persevere and keep moving forward.

It took 3 years to turn around but, by the fourth year, tremendous gains had been made. Pass rates had climbed above the national average. Applications for admission to the school had risen by 10 percent, and student satisfaction, both upon exiting the school and one year later, were at an all-time high. Anthony had succeeded and even had attracted the attention of administrators, who publicly recognized him at the university graduation that next fall for his innovative work.

Readiness and Reflection

1. * From the following list of traits, mark those you feel you possess:

_____ sensitive	_____ intuitive	_____ sense of destiny
_____ original	_____ adaptable	_____ ingenious
_____ flexible	_____ energetic	_____ observant
_____ imaginative	_____ confident	_____ persistent
_____ risk-taker	_____ resourceful	_____ self-disciplined
_____ independent	_____ perceive things differently from others	
_____ open-minded	_____ able to challenge people and situations	
_____ curious	_____ visionary (sees possibilities)	
_____ sense of humor	_____ synthesizes information correctly	
_____ able to fantasize	_____ inquisitive (asks questions)	
_____ divergent thinker	_____ self-knowledgeable	
_____ non-conforming	_____ tolerant of ambiguity	

Add up how many you marked. The more you marked, the more creative you are. Create a plan for how you will develop those you did not mark.

*Adapted from Black, R.A. (2006). Cre8ting people, places and possibilities. Retrieved August 5, 2008, from www.cre8ng.com.

2. Invite your team to a "Discover My Creative Side" retreat. Ask each member of your team to write down an experience in which they did something totally new and different. As the stories are told, listeners write down what they hear as the creative elements of the story. The group then discusses these elements and identifies ways the team member can continue to use or reawaken creativity.

3. Discuss organizational rules with your team members, asking them to identify the three rules they would most like to break. Then, discuss the principle behind the rule, and encourage participants to identify how the principle could be applied in a more appealing way.

4. Ask each person to write down all thoughts about a particularly perplexing issue facing the team. Then do a round-robin sharing, writing down all ideas. Ask them to group the ideas by similarity. After reflecting on the honed list, ask if there are any other ideas. Have the group identify the top 10 ideas for further discussion, then the top six, and finally the top three. Gain group consensus on the three best ways to develop an innovation that solves the issue.

5. Create three task forces to develop a plan for taking the three ideas to innovative action.

6. Reflect on what you have learned in this chapter and from the exercise responses. Write one paragraph on where you see your creative and innovative self today.

7. Develop two strategies to improve your creativity and innovation, and add them to your leadership development plan.

Chapter 14

Can't Do It Without You: Humility and Recognition

The importance of humility as a desirable trait blasted onto the leadership scene when Collins (2001) wrote about leaders of good to great organizations. Collins' research—spanning more than 15 years—revealed that great companies are led by Level 5 leaders—people who demonstrated, across the board, a unique blend of a strong, fearless will and a modest, humble manner. This discovery led Collins to dig deeper into the characteristics, process, benefits, and disadvantages of being such a leader, and his model reportedly has been quite successful.

The Humble Leader

Humility is an overlooked attribute in leadership, seldom talked about or taught. Humility is the opposite of arrogance and narcissism. Humble leaders know they are not inherently superior to others. They neither debase nor exalt themselves, but simply recognize all people as equal in value.

Most successful leaders understand that humility is essential to winning hearts and minds. For people to follow, the leader must visibly demonstrate caring and concern. Leaders continually show their respect toward people and demonstrate a powerful commitment to achieve results for their organizations.

"Humility is the opposite of arrogance and narcissism. Humble leaders know they are not inherently superior to others."

Humble leaders are ambitious for their people and organization, working to bring out the best in both. Rarely do they allow their egos to interfere with their decisions and actions. Their primary concern is for the success of the organization. They channel their ego needs away from themselves and into building a better organization. It is not that these leaders have no ego or self-interest. In fact, they are incredibly ambitious, but their ambition is for the organization, not themselves (Collins, 2004).

Leaders who display humility seldom take credit for their organization's success, being quick to attribute achievements to subordinates. They readily and frequently recognize that they and their organization could not possibly have achieved greatness without the people who helped fulfill the vision. In fact, they experience great joy and satisfaction from watching people succeed, grow, and develop themselves and the organization.

Over the course of time, humble leaders have led movements to overcome injustice: Consider Nelson Mandela and his selflessness in achieving equality in South Africa. They have led nations: Consider Franklin Roosevelt, who led America through a great war to an era of prosperity. They have led small groups in the workplace: Consider Dame Cicely Saunders, a cancer-care nurse, social worker, and medical doctor who conceived and led the modern hospice-care movement. These individuals had a strong will to succeed for their cause and the humility to know they could not do it alone.

Humility as an Essential Element

Humility, in its truest form, does not allow leaders to lose sight of their humanness. It keeps them attuned to their frailties, vulnerabilities, and inadequacies. Humility keeps the ego in check, so it doesn't interfere with the greater good that leaders seek. This does not mean leaders are without ego; in fact, humble leaders have very strong egos and are quite self-confident. Their humility actually strengthens their confidence. They draw significance and satisfaction not from and for themselves, but rather from and for others. They feel more confident, knowing they have the support, expertise, and resources of others around them.

Humble leaders have little need to brag or attribute success to their own efforts. Instead, they willingly give credit to those around them. As Collins says, when talking about results, the humble leader points out the window to others. But when things go bad, they point to themselves in the mirror (Collins, 2001).

Leaders look for humility in the people they work with. Of great importance to leaders is finding people who share the same values as the leader and the organization. They look for people who possess not only expertise and competence but, more importantly, character. In fact, for most, character is non-negotiable.

The demeanor of a humble leader is characterized as quiet, modest, reserved, gracious, mild-mannered, and understated. This mode of behavior is authentic and in no way constitutes false modesty. True humility is counter-cultural—i.e., the opposite of the rather prevalent me-first philosophy of society—which explains why humility is so unusual. Great leaders master their vanity and themselves.

Cultivating Humility

No one gets up in the morning and says, "Boy, I am going to be humble today!" This trait is cultivated over time and demonstrated by leaders. By setting the example, leaders move their followers in the same direction they take, and through similar behaviors. Telling people they must be humble or motivated is rather insulting. The best way to beget a trait that is valued is by living it daily, as an example for others.

Cultivating humility requires the leader to be magnanimous and give credit where it is due. It is about being gracious in failure and defeat, and allowing others who are defeated to retain their dignity. Magnanimous leaders credit people with successes and assume personal responsibility for failures.

Humility in Action

Nina was a modest and humble person. As vice president for new product development for a large pharmaceutical company, she was also quite successful. Her health care background gave her an edge in understanding the company's customer base, but her humility won her more successes. She always spoke of her successes in terms of the collective "we." She unfailingly attributed her achievements to her team but, when products didn't produce anticipated results, she was quick to say that she needed to analyze the situation, as she had obviously missed something important.

When pressed to talk about her contributions, Nina's responses ran the gamut from "I don't think I can take much credit for that," to "We are so fortunate to have talented people working here." There was never a hint of self-aggrandizing or boastfulness, only self-effacing understatement. Yet, she had tremendous ambition and drive to succeed, and she continually challenged team members to think, create, and produce more efficiently. Her team responded with nimbleness and quality, mostly because they knew she was working with them.

It is not easy being humble, but the benefits can be great. Humility produces a high level of trust and allows the leader to achieve exceptional, lasting results. Here are other benefits (Armour, 2007):

- Humility allows us to rid ourselves of concern about being the hub of attention. When people step aside and let others shine, they are communicating respect, value, and regard for them. This increases trust.

- Humility leaves people open to what they can learn from others. The result is increased wisdom and expertise, because they have many mentors.

- Humility allows us to treat even difficult people with respect and help them feel more worthwhile. A humble leader has turned around many naysayers and critics by making them feel significant.

- Humility engenders a spirit of gratitude, helping us to keep a positive outlook on life and work.

- Humility enables us to face our own failings and learn valuable lessons from them.

- Humility helps us be more patient with people.

- Humility makes leaders approachable and receptive. It also fosters accountability.

- Humility keeps curiosity alive for, in being aware that we don't know it all, exploration and learning can occur.

In many ways, humility puts into proper perspective our pride about who we are, our achievements, and our worth. It is about the quiet confidence of our human nature. Leaders take pride in the work of those around them for the greater good, and they have confidence in their abilities. Humble leaders bring out the best in others and constantly strive to do that in themselves.

Readiness and Reflections

1. For the following statements, answer "true" or "false":

   _____ In general, I think what others have to say is as good as, or better than, what I have to say.

   _____ I don't need to always get my own way.

   _____ I readily admit when I am not right.

   _____ When I am right, I don't need to point it out to people.

   _____ I give my opinion honestly when asked.

   _____ I learn from others' point of view.

   _____ I believe credit should be given to those who do the work.

   _____ I seldom make excuses for my decisions and actions.

   _____ I am willing to do whatever it takes to get the job done.

   _____ I am honest about my faults.

   _____ I think about the lasting effect I can have in my work.

   _____ I am happy for people when they receive promotions, recognition, and esteem from others.

   _____ I am regarded as a caring and compassionate person.

   _____ My self-confidence comes from my own self-understanding, not from what others think.

   _____ My primary concern at work is for the people and organization I serve.

   The more you entered "true," the more humble you are.

2. Reflect on the statements to which you responded "false." Consider what you do or think that makes that statement false. What could you do to change this?

3. Make it a daily habit to do a menial task at work.

4. When having a conversation with others at work, note how many times you refer to yourself versus your team.

5. Have a conversation with your team about what it means to give credit where credit is due.

6. Converse with a friend or mentor about the meaning of being humble at work. What do they see in their work environment that encourages or discourages humility? What do you see in your work environment?

7. Reflect on what you have learned from this chapter and about yourself through the exercises. Write a paragraph about where you see yourself today with regard to being a humble leader.

8. Develop two strategies for becoming more humble, and add them to your personal leadership development plan.

Chapter 15

Let's Party! Recognition and Celebration

Leading a group of people to success, with purpose, requires diverse traits and behaviors. Leadership involves complex relationships and interactions. Leaders who invest in their people and organizations highly desire continuation of success, even after they are gone.

They wish to instill the values and beliefs of the shared vision into everyone's work, so the work can be replicated and continue seamlessly. They want motivation, inspiration, and empowerment to become second nature to people and a vital part of the organization's culture. A sure way to achieve this integration is through recognition and celebration of the work, the people, and the values.

Recognition

Recognition is about forming an environment in which everyone's contributions are noticed and appreciated. It is not only about acknowledging the good results that have occurred, but also about appreciating the effort and expertise of people. Recognition reinforces positive behaviors, as well as performance.

"Recognition is about forming an environment in which everyone's contributions are noticed and appreciated."

When people put forward their best effort, working intently on behalf of the organization's vision, they need encouragement and emotional replenishment. By recognizing contributions of individual team members, leaders encourage and motivate people to continue their efforts. Through recognition, leaders stimulate and inspire their team's internal drive (Kouzes & Posner, 2007).

 ## Re-energizing Through Recognition

Samantha led a team that consistently performed at a high level. As director of technology for a large not-for-profit, she recognized that staff members were constantly bombarded with requests for their expertise in designing, programming, and data mining. At the same time, they were undertaking a large data conversion of all the organization's files into an integrated system.

Samantha and her team had been planning and communicating this change for months and, despite a few post-conversion glitches, the process went better than anticipated. However, the team was wiped out physically and emotionally. Samantha did several things to re-energize them. She asked the CEO to publicly acknowledge the group effort in the successful conversion. She surprised her team by taking them to lunch and a movie one afternoon. And, she arranged for each of them to have an extra day off for rest, relaxation, and reflection during the week after the conversion. Team members not only were grateful for the recognition, but also were impressed by Samantha's concern, and they appreciated her consideration of their work and feelings. After the day of rest, each returned to work feeling rejuvenated and recommitted to the work and the team.

Genuine and Purposeful Recognition

Leaders expect the best of themselves and the people they lead. They have high expectations for performance that others strive to attain. Great leaders bring the work of others to life—not only because the leaders believe in the capabilities of others, but also because they care deeply for them (Kouzes & Posner, 2007). Recognition must reflect this care and belief.

Leaders make recognition significant to the individual. They set high expectations and reward high performance and, in addition, help people focus on what is important and establish individual goals. These goals become the focal point for individual expectations and performance.

On the journey to goal completion, people need to know they are making progress, so leaders take the opportunity—often—to provide feedback. The feedback should be personal and related to the individual's contribution to his or her goal, as well as the common goal. This type of feedback is significant, because it relates specifically to the person, yet illuminates his or her contribution to the larger picture.

In recognizing people, leaders avoid the predictable and the routine. This does not mean that organization-wide recognitions are not appreciated. What it does mean is that this type of recognition is not enough to replenish people's desire to meet expectations and be high performers. For that, a personal approach is needed, and that means the leader has to invest in and get to know members of his or her team (Heathfield, 2008).

Leaders do this by paying attention and developing relationships with the members of their team. It means understanding what members like and dislike. It means being available and sometimes walking the halls just to say hello and chat. It means taking an interest in and learning about people and what makes them tick. Once leaders know the people on their team, they become more creative and personal in tangibly recognizing their contributions and providing incentives.

Personalized Recognition

Chris was a well-liked and respected director of professional develop-ment at a hospital. She and her team of eight managed the continuing education needs for 1,200 nurses. Chris knew how lost she would be without her team members and regularly told them so. She also had quite high expectations of them and demanded quality results.

One of the goals of the chief nursing officer was to implement evidence-based practice within the nursing-practice model, and she entrusted Chris and her team with developing an implementation strategy and education plan.

Chris and her team labored for 6 months in developing the plan. They spent countless hours surveying and assessing the nurses' attitudes and needs, and clocked many hours holding focus groups and researching models that other institutions used. Along the way, Chris hosted pizza parties to say thanks to staff members for their hard work. Periodically, they had "kick back and relax afternoons" at a local park or shopping mall, where they talked about anything but work.

During these nonwork conversations, Chris would ask team members about themselves, their families, and their biggest self-indulgence. She took an interest in them, and they in her, developing a camaraderie that few had experienced before. When their work plan was complete and accepted by the administration, Chris brought each of her team members a personal gift of thanks.

Each gift had something to do with the team member's personal indulgence. One loved chocolates, so Chris gave her a box of them. Another enjoyed environmental ambience music, so Chris gave her a CD of ocean sounds. Still another enjoyed gardening, so Chris gave her a perennial for her garden. In the end, it was not the gifts that mattered most; it was Chris' recognition of their very hard work in such a genuine, personalized way.

How leaders recognize teams and team members can vary widely. One should never underestimate the power of saying a simple "thank you," or stopping by to tell someone what a great job he or she did. Sometimes, in the busyness of work, we are so relieved that a project has been completed that we quickly move on to the next project.

A great leader takes time to stop and revel in the success, recognizing in a highly personal way every individual's contribution to that success. These acts make people feel good about themselves and their work, and stimulate their willingness to go the extra mile. Recognition encourages positive, performance-enhancing attitudes and behaviors, something money can't buy.

Learning From Successes and Failures

Collective reflection is a strategy that all great leaders use. Because leaders, in the best interest of the team and organization, continually strive to do things better, they spend time reflecting on the dynamics of a goal completed. By themselves and with their team, they do a postmortem on the project, task, or goal that has been achieved.

They examine the process, interactions, and interdependencies that were necessary to make it happen. Leaders put their "what-if" hats back on and query: "What if we had done it this way, or what if we had engaged this group? Would our result have been better?" In essence, through reflection, they learn from their lived experience, so they can replicate and improve their results. They also lead their team through failures. As painful as this may be for some, there is great value in examining and defining what went wrong, so the process can be improved.

 Learning From Failure

John was team leader for a project to develop an e-commerce site for his organization. After much anticipation and years of planning, the site delivered about half the revenue anticipated by the team. John and members of the team analyzed what had gone awry and went back to the drawing board to repurpose the site.

They discovered several factors that contributed to less-than-optimal performance: The administration was not very supportive of the project or its development costs; co-workers were not clear about their contribution to goals established for the site; and end users were not accustomed to this type of service from John's organization—it was a culture change.

In retooling the site, John entered into a contract of support with the administration. He increased communication about the progress he and his team were making. Most importantly, he talked and listened extensively to end users about their needs and desires. As a result, he and his team learned from their failure.

Celebration

Celebrations at team and organizational levels are important to creating a spirit of cohesiveness, collaboration, and community. This culture of celebration fuels unity and stimulates motivation within an individual, whether he or she is the center of attention or not. A leader who ignores or puts up barriers to organizational celebrations, or considers them frivolous and costly, is ignoring the basic human need to feel worthy. Celebrations are exclamation points that mark passage of something significant—something that has made a difference. To deny this is to deny value and worth to the common good.

Celebrations are important for the long-term health of an organization, because they proclaim respect and gratitude, renew a sense of together-ness, and remind everyone of values and history. Celebrations bond people together and create community. They provide a chance to acknowledge and renew commitment (Kouzes & Posner, 2007, Heathfield, 2008). In the end, being a great leader boils down to using competencies, skills, and traits to develop and sustain relationships. People naturally gravitate toward those with whom they feel a personal connection. That is why leaders become personally involved and invested in those they work with.

Great leaders strive to make employees part of organizational life and thus insist that accolades are also given publicly. Private accolades are healthy for the individual, but public accolades are healthy for the organization. In showcasing and acknowledging people publicly, the leader places the spotlight on real-life examples of what the organization values. These public celebrations are an opportunity to tell stories of success that demonstrate fulfillment of organizational values—thus encouraging others to follow suit.

 ## Celebrating Collaboration

Nan was the head of an organization whose staff members had developed the habit of working in silos, often at cross and duplicative purposes with one another. Collaboration and teamwork were values she held dear. Once the decision was made to establish collaborative work practices, staff spent many hours attending workshops in preparation for implementing the new approach.

To show the value and success of teamwork, Nan wanted to recognize team members who had worked collaboratively, across departments, to complete an initiative or project. Only one team was honored that year at the staff recognition event, but the celebration was grand. The next year, there were five teams and, by the third year, too many to single out one. It was clear that the desired value had become integrated into the organization's culture.

Leaders understand that celebrations also provide social support for people—a time to come together in a social atmosphere, meet new people, and get to know others better. Socializing with others can stimulate working with them across the organization. This can be rejuvenating, even fun.

Fun at work is not an oxymoron. In fact, a relaxed, enjoyable atmosphere sustains productivity and gives people a sense of well-being. It also fosters a sense of connectedness.

Fun at Work

Lee was a light-hearted fellow and, even though his work as a financial officer at a not-for-profit organization was serious, he found ways to make what could be tedious, stressful work more enjoyable for his team. Lee was quite a good cook, so once a month, he came to work early and fixed breakfast for his team. They sat in their conference room, furnished with easy chairs and a sofa, and enjoyed pancakes and sausage. While Lee didn't plan it, the conversation eventually came around to work. They talked about issues, processes, and the team's role in the organization. Lee said some of the department's best ideas came from their breakfasts together.

Celebrations reinforce the fact that exceptional results and successes are the products of performance by many. By basing celebrations on key values and beliefs, the leader reinforces what is important for people to focus on. Celebrating builds connectedness and demonstrates the leader's investment in people on the journey to excellence.

Leadership is about impact. Leaders, by the smallest of actions, have significant influence on others at every level of a group or organization. Their behavior creates the culture and builds the framework for responding to change, challenges, and uncertainty that face all people and organizations (Porter-O'Grady & Malloch, 2002).

Readiness and Reflection

1. Rate yourself on the following statements with

   1 = I rarely do this

   2 = I occasionally do this

   3 = I regularly do this

   _____ Have a formal way to publicly acknowledge the contributions of my team to the organization.

   _____ Plan and carry out surprise thank-yous for my team.

   _____ Communicate regularly the progress my team has made toward our goals.

   _____ Enjoy getting to know the people I work with better.

   _____ Engage in collective reflection with my team.

   _____ Find valuable learning in both success and failure.

   _____ Enjoy, encourage, schedule, and participate in celebrations.

   _____ Encourage others when things are not going well for them.

   _____ Find creative, personal ways to reward the successes of my team.

   _____ Have fun at work.

Add up your scores. If you scored 1-14, consider what you personally can do to be more in touch with your team and acknowledge their contributions. If you scored 15-24, you are doing a nice job of making your team feel significant and valued. Expand your repertoire of recognition and celebration tools. If you scored 25-30, everyone must want to come and work with you, because you are so good at making people feel they are making a huge difference for the organization, while having fun.

2. Think back to a time when you were recognized for a contribution to your organization. Why was this so memorable? What was done that made it significant? How did it make you feel? Afterward, how did it affect your work? Jot down your thoughts.

3. In a meeting with your team members, have them tell the story of their most significant recognition. As a group, discuss common elements in the stories.

4. Plan a surprise, fun activity for your team in the next 2 weeks.

5. Post a "Thank-You" bulletin board in a central place your team sees every day. Give everyone thank-you cards, and encourage them to post thank-yous to others on the board. You should be the first to post your thanks.

6. Reflect on what you have learned from the chapter and about yourself in your responses to these exercises. Write one paragraph about where you see yourself today in recognition and celebration competency.

7. Develop two strategies to improve your recognition and celebration skills and add these to your personal leadership development plan.

Epilogue

Anyone can be a leader. All it takes is desire, determination, and a clear sense of who you are and where you want to go. Everyone can make a difference in his or her work and life. Never let anyone tell you differently. Leadership is learned, not something you were born with. As Kouzes and Posner (2007) say: "We're all born. What we do with what we have before we die is up to us" (p. 339).

> *Leadership is learned, not something you were born with.*

Because leadership is actually self-development, throughout this book you have been encouraged to reflect on what you have learned about yourself. You have also been encouraged to think about self-improvement. As you continue this inner quest, here is the final "Readiness and Reflection" exercise.

On a blank sheet of paper, make four columns. At the top of the first column on the left-hand side of the paper, write "Trait." Moving right across the page, label the next column "Strategies," the next column "Actions," and the final column "When." Now, begin to fill in the columns, using the 15 traits in this book and the two self-improvement strategies you developed for each trait. Add two actions for each of your strategies, and give yourself a date—or time frame—for completion. A sample is below.

Trait	Strategies	Actions	When
Recognition/Celebration	1. Regularly recognize my team's contributions.	1. Have a surprise thank-you event.	1. Next week
	2. Get to know my team better.	2. Spend 10 minutes a day with a different team member talking about their interests.	2. Over the next month

Once you have completed this last exercise, your personal leadership development plan is before you.

Now, you are ready, set … go lead!

References and Readings for Additional Leadership Development

Preface *References*

Bennis, W.G. (2003). *On becoming a leader* (Rev. ed.). Cambridge, MA: Perseus Books Group.

Bennis, W.G. & Goldsmith, J. (2003). *Learning to lead: A workbook on becoming a leader*. New York: Basic Books.

Additional Leadership Development Resources

Dickenson-Hazard, N. (2004). Cultivating effective leadership skills for nurses: A commentary. *Policy, politics and Nursing Practice*, 5 (3), 145-146.

The Institute for Innovation, Integration & Impact, Inc. (2008). Leadership readiness assessment. Retrieved on June 24, 2008, from http://www.prismltd.com/leader.htm

Northouse, P.G. (2007). *Leadership: Theory and practice*. Thousand Oaks, CA: Sage Publications.

Sanborn, M. (2006). *You don't need a title to be a leader*. New York: Doubleday.

Tourangeau, A.E. & McGilton, K. (2004). Measuring leadership practices of nurses using the leadership practices inventory. *Nursing Research* 53 (3), 182-189.

Chapter 1 *References*

Drucker, P. (1996). Not enough generals were killed. In Hesselbein, F., Goldsmith, M., & Beckhard, R. (Eds.), *The leader of the future*. San Francisco: Jossey-Bass.

Klein, E. (2006). *You are the leader you've been waiting for*. Encinitas, CA: Wisdom Heart Press Book.

Prism LTD, (2008). *Leadership: Developing people*. Retrieved on June 25, 2008 from http://www.prismltd.com/leader.htm.

Quinn, R.E. (2004). *Building the bridge as you walk on it*. San Francisco, CA: Jossey-Bass.

Additional Leadership Development Resources

Buckingham, M. & Clifton, D. (2001). *Now, discover your strengths*. New York: The Free Press.

Buckingham, M. (2007). *Go put your strengths to work*. New York: The Free Press.

Heifeitz, R. & Linsky, M. (2002). *Leadership on the line*. Boston, MA: Harvard Business School Press.

Jacques, A. (2008). The life-work integrity assessment. Retrieved 26 August 2008 from http://www.healthyworkplaceweek.ca/pdf/Individual_Activity.pdf

Johannsen, M. (2008). Nine characteristics of successful entrepreneurs and business leaders. Retrieved on June 25, 2008 from http://www.legacee.com/Info/Leadership/LeadershipEntrepreneurial.html

Leider, R. (2005). *The power of purpose: Creating meaning in your life and work*. San Francisco: Berrett-Koehler Publishers.

Myatt, M (2008). Leaders vs managers. Retrieved June 25, 2008 from http://www.n2growth.com/blog/?p=24

Palmer, P. (1999). *Let your life speak: Listening for the voice of vocation.* San Francisco: Jossey-Bass.

Rath, T. & Clifton, D. (2007). *How full is your bucket?* New York: Gallup Press.

Chapter 2 *References*

Cashman, K. (2008). *Authentic leadership.* Retrieved June 23, 2008 from http://www.winstonbrill.com/bril001/html/article_index/articles/301-350/article305_body.html

Cohen, A. (2008). *What is authentic leadership?* Retrieved 26 August 2008 from http://www.andrewcohen.org/andrew/authentic-leadership.asp

George, B. (2004). *Truly authentic leadership.* Retrieved August 26, 2008 from http://www.usnews.com/usnews/news/articles/061022/30authentic_print.htm

Powell, C. L. (1995). *My American journey.* New York: Ballantine Books.

Quinn, R.E. (2004). *Building the bridge as you walk on it.* San Francisco, CA: Jossey-Bass.

Additional Leadership Development Resource

Authenticity Consulting, LLC: www.actionlearningcentral.com/

Authenticity Consulting, LLC: www.authenticleadership.com

George, B. (2003). *Authentic leadership: Rediscovering the secrets to creating lasting values.* San Francisco, CA: Jossey-Bass.

McNamara, C. (2008). *Field guide to leadership and supervision.* Minneapolis, MN: Authenticity Consulting, LLC.

Authentic Leadership Institute: www.authleadership.com

True North Leaders: Retrieved June 25, 2008, www.truenorthleaders.com

Chapter 3 *References*

Cathy, S.T. (2002). *Eat mor chikin:Inspire more people.* Decatur, GA: Looking Glass Books.

Kouzes, J.M. & Posner, B.Z. (2007). *The leadership challenge.* San Francisco, CA: Jossey-Bass.

Kouzes, J.M. & Posner, B.Z. (2006). *A leader's legacy.* San Francisco, CA: Jossey-Bass.

Secretan, L. (2000). *Reclaiming higher ground.* Canada: Macmillan Publishing.

Additional Leadership Development Resources

De Pree, M. (2003). *Leading without power: Finding hope in serving community.* San Francisco, CA: Jossey-Bass.

Friedman, S.D. (2008). *Total leadership: Be a better leader, have a richer life.* Boston, MA: Harvard Business School Publishing.

Leadership Turn: www.leadershipturn.com

The Secretan Center: http://www.secretan.com/

Tom Peters Company: http://tompeters.com/

Chapter 4 *References*

Bennis, W.G. (2003). *On becoming a leader* (Rev.Ed.). Cambridge, MA: Perseus Books Group.

Additional Leadership Development Resources

Covey Community. Retrieved June 26, 2008 from www.stephencovey.com

Covey, S.R. (2006). *The 8th habit: From effectiveness to greatness.* New York: Simon & Schuster, Inc.

De Pree, M. (2004). *Leadership is an art.* New York: Doubleday.

Gilbert, D. (2007). *Stumbling on happiness.* Boston, MA: Harvard Business School Press.

Human Performance Institute: http://www.lgeperformance.com/

Leider, R.J. & Shapiro, D.A. (1995). *Repacking your bags.* San Francisco, CA: Berrett-Koehler Publishers.

Loehr, J. (2007). *The power of story.* New York: Simon & Schuster, Inc. Performance Programs, Inc. Retrieved June 26, 2008 from http://www.lgeperformance.com/book_power_of_story.html

Maxwell, J.C. (2008). *Leadership gold: Lessons I've learned from a lifetime of leading.* Nashville, TN: Thomas Nelson, Inc.

Chapter 5 *References*

Bennis, W.G. (2003). *On becoming a leader* (Rev. ed.). Cambridge, MA: Perseus Books Group.

Bennis, W.G. & Nanus, B. (2007). *Leaders: Strategies for taking charge.* New York: HarperCollins Publishers, Inc.

Collins, J. (2001). *Good to great.* New York: HarperCollins Publisher, Inc.

Kouzes, J.M. & Posner, B. Z. (2007). *The leadership challenge.* San Francisco, CA: Jossey-Bass.

Matusak, L.R. (1997). *Finding your voice.* San Francisco, CA: Jossey-Bass.

Quinn, R.E. (2004). *Building the bridge as you walk on it.* San Francisco, CA: Jossey-Bass.

Additional Leadership Development Resources

Canton, J. (2006). *The extreme future.* New York: Penguin Group.

Cornish, E. (2004). *Futuring: The exploration of the future.* Bethesda, MD: World Futures Society.

Future Health Care: www.futurehealthcareus.com

Gardner, H. (2006). *Five minds of the future.* Boston, MA: Harvard Business School Publishing.

Healthcare Futures: www.ourhealthcarefuture.org

Penn, M.J. (2007). *Microtrends.* New York: Hachette Book Group, Inc.

World Futures Society: www.wfs.org

Chapter 6 *References*

Baldoni, J. (2005). *Great motivation secrets of great leaders.* New York: McGraw-Hill Publishing.

Clark, D. (2008). *Motivation and leadership.* Retrieved June 26, 2008 from www.nwlink.com

Kouzes, J.M. & Posner, B. Z. (2003).*The leadership challenge workbook.* San Francisco, CA: Jossey-Bass.

Mage, G. (2008). *How leaders can motivate people*. Retrieved 26 August 2008 from http://www.makingitwork.com

Webster's New World Dictionary of the American Language (2004). New York; The World Publishing Company.

Additional Leadership Development Resources

The Center for Contemplative Mind in Society: http://www.contemplativemind.org/

Farsight Leadership: www.farsightleadership.com/

Follow Your Dreams: www.followyourdreams.com/food.html

Sheehan, J.K. (2007). *A leader becomes a leader: Inspirational stories of leadership for a new generation*. Belmont, MA: True Gifts Publishing.

The Happy Guy: www.thehappyguy.com/l/daily-motivation-inspiration.php

Tracy, B. (2006). How to become a motivational leader. *Leader's Edge* 1(9). Retrieved June 26, 2008 from www.amanet.org/LeadersEdge/editorial.cfm?Ed=323

Chapter 7 *References*

Baldoni, J. (2003). *Great communication secrets of great leaders*. New York, MrGraw-Hill.

Barrett, D.J. (2005). *Leadership Communication*. New York: Irwin Professional Publishing.

DeVito, J.A. (2007). *Essentials of human communication*. Glenview, Il: Longman Publishing Group.

Matusak, L.R. (1997). *Finding your voice*. San Francisco, Ca: Jossey-Bass.

Additional Leadership Development Resources

Communication Styles: www.nsba.org/sbot/toolkit/CommStyl.html

Communication Test: www.queendom.com/tests/access_page/index.htm?idRegTest=683

Dickenson-Hazard, N. & Root, J. (2000). Communicating effectively in Bower, F.L. (ed) *Nurses taking the lead: Personal qualities of effective leadership*. Philadelphia, PA: W.B. Saunders Company.

Kegan, R. & Lahey, L (2001). *How the way we talk can change the way we work: Seven languages for transformation*. San Francisco, CA: Jossey-Bass.

Scott, S. (2002). *Fierce conversations: Achieving success at work and in life, one conversation at a time*. New York: Viking Press.

Stone, D., Patton, B. & Heen, S. (1999). *Difficult conversations: How to discuss what matters most*. New York: Viking Press.

The Positive Way: www.positive-way.com/communic.htm

Chapter 8 *References*

Klein, E. (2002). *Co-mentoring in healthcare*. Encinitas, CA: Wisdom Heart Press.

Klein, E. (2000). *You are the leader you've been waiting for: Enjoying high performance and high fulfillment at work*. Encinitas, CA: Wisdom Heart Press.

Kouzes, J.M., Posner, B.Z. (2007). *The leadership challenge*. San Francisco, CA: Jossey-Bass.

Merton, R.K. (1993). *On the shoulders of Giants*. Chicago, IL:University of Chicago Press.

Schwarzkopf, H.N. (1993). *It doesn't take a hero: The autobiography of General Norman Schwarzkopf.* New York: Bantam Books.

Vance, C. & Olson, R.K. (1998). *The mentor connection in nursing.* New York: Springer Publishing Company.

Additional Leadership Development Resources

About Management: http://management.about.com/cs/people/a/mentoring.htm

Center for Coaching and Mentoring: www.coachingandmentoring.com/ccmFreeResources.htm

Ensher, E. & Murphy, S. (2005). *Power mentoring: How successful mentors and protégés get the most out of their relationship.* San Francisco, CA: Jossey-Bass.

Free Management Library: www.managementhelp.org/guiding/mentrng/mentrng.htm

Johnson, B. & Ridley, C. (2004). *The elements of mentoring.* New York: Palgrave Macmillian.

U.S. Department of Education: http://www.ed.gov/pubs/OR/ConsumerGuides/mentor.html

U.S. Department of Education Mentoring Resource Center: www.edmentoring.org/

Chapter 9 *References*

Bell, C.R. & Bell, B.R. (2003). Empowerment is a leadership trick! *Innovative leader* 12(10). Retrieved June 16, 2008 from http://www.winstonbrill.com/bril001/html/article_index/articles/551-600/article586_body.html

Block, P. (1996). *Stewardship:Choosing service over self interest.* San Francisco, CA: Berrett-Koehler Publishers, Inc.

Hutson, D. (2002). *Best practices of empowering leaders.* Retrieved 26 August 2008 from http://www.frogpond.com/printversion.cfm?artcled=dhutson07

Kouses, J.M. & Posner, B.Z. (2007). *The leadership challenge.* San Francisco, CA: Jossey-Bass.

Kouzes, J.M. & Posner, B.Z. (2002). *The leadership challenge workbook.* San Francisco, CA: Jossey-Bass.

Mind Tools. (2008). *Successful delegation.* Retrieved June 16, 2008 from Http://www.mindtools.com/pages/article/newLDR_98.htm

Winter, G. & Klein, E. (2005). *To do or not to do: How successful leaders make better decisions.* Encinitas, CA: Wisdom Heart Press.

Additional Leadership Development Resources

Blanchard, K. (2003). *Servant leader.* Nashville, TN: Thomas Nelson, Inc.

Block, P. (1987). *The empowered manager.* San Francisco, CA: Jossey-Bass.

Designed Learning. Retrieved 26 August 2008 from www.designedlearning.com/index.htm

Klein, E. & Izzo, J.B. (2003). *Awakening the corporate soul: Four paths to unleash the power of people at work.* Canada: Fairwinds Publishing.

Maxwell, J.C. (2007). *The 21 irrefutable laws of leadership: Follow them and people will follow you.* Nashville, TN: Thomas Nelson, Inc.

Maxwell, J.C. (2004). *Winning with people.* Nashville, TN: Thomas Nelson, Inc.

Personal Empowerment Resources. Retrieved 26 August 2008 from www.empowermentresources.com/page6.html

Chapter 10 *References*

Bennis, W.G., Goleman, D., & O'Toole, J. (2008). *Transparency: How leaders create a culture of candor*. San Francisco, CA: Jossey-Bass.

Kouzes, J.M. & Posner, B.Z. (2002). *The leadership challenge workbook*, San Francisco, CA: Jossey-Bass.

Porter-O'Grady, T. & Malloch, K. (2002). *Quantum leadership*. Gaithersburg, MD: Aspen Publications.

Willard, M., Hitchcock, D. (2008). *Accountability is a sticky subject for teams*. Retrieved June 16, 2008 from http://www.teambuildinginc.com/article_team_accountability.htm

Additional Leadership Development Resources

Accountability Central: www.accountability-central.com/transparency-disclosure/transparency-disclosure-intro/

Education Leadership Tool Kit: www.nsba.org/sbot/toolkit/Accountability.html

Russo, E. M. (2008). *Solving the puzzle of team accountability*. Retrieved 26 August 2008 from www.hrdq.com/content/articles/article7.htm

Safe Families Accountability Tool. Retrieved 26 August 2008 from www.safefamilies.org/dailycheckin.php

UB Resource Centre. *Accountability and Transparency for Health*. Retrieved 26 August 2008 from www.bu.edu/actforhealth/research.htm

Chapter 11 *References*

Abaris Consulting (2001). *Organizational Change Readiness*. London, Ontario Abaris Consulting.

Calvert, G. (1993). *Highwire management*. San Francisco, CA: Jossey-Bass.

Duck, J. D. (2001). *The change monster*. New York: Three Rivers Press.

Kotter, J. P. (1996). *Leading change*. Boston, MA: Harvard Business School Press.

Kotter, J. P. (2002). *The heart of change*. Boston, MA: Harvard Business School Press.

Kouzes, J. M. & Posner, B. Z. (2007). *The leadership challenge*. San Francisco, CA: Jossey-Bass.

Malmeister, L. (2000). Taking a risk in *Nurses taking the lead*. Bower,F. (ed.) Philadelphia, PA: W.B. Saunders.

Matusak, L. R. (1997). *Finding Your Voice*. San Francisco, CA: Jossey-Bass.

Maurer, R. (1996). *Beyond the wall of resistence*. Austin, TX: Bard Press.

Myatt, M. (2007). *Leadership matters*. Parker, CO: Outskirts Press.

Scott, C.D. & Jaffe, D. (2004). *Managing personal change*. Menlo Park, CA: Crisp Publications.

Additional Leadership Development Resources

Change Management Center: http://www.change-management.com/

Change Management Resources: http://www.beyondresistance.com/

Harvard Business Review Paperback Series. (2007). *Leading through change*. Boston, MA: Harvard Business School Press.

Managing Change Guide. Retrieved June 28, 2008 from www.oursouthwest.com/SusBus/mggchange.html

Chapter 12 *References*

Buckingham, M. & Clifton, D. (2001). *Now, discover your strengths*. New York: The Free Press.

Mintzberg, H. (1994). *The rise and fall of strategic planning*. New York: The Free Press.

Pietersen, W. (2002). *Reinventing strategy*. New York: John Wiley & Sons, Inc.

Dees, J. G., Emerson, J. & Economy, P. (2002). *Strategic tools for social entrepreneurs*. New York: John Wiley & Sons, Inc.

Additional Leadership Development Resources

About.com: Human Resources: http://humanresources.about.com/od/strategicplanning1/Strategic_Planning_Resources.htm

Birnbaum, B. (2004). *Strategic thinking: A four piece puzzle*. Costa Mesa, Ca: Douglas Mountain Publishing.

Free Management Library: www.managementhelp.org/plan_dec/str_plan/str_plan.htm

Haines, S.G. (2007). *The top 10 everyday tools for strategic thinking*. San Diego, CA: Systems Thinking Press.

Hughes, R.L. & Beatty, K.M. (2005). *Becoming a strategic leader: Your role in your organization's enduring success*. San Francisco, CA: Jossey-Bass.

Ken Blanchard Companies: www.kenblanchard.com/Search/Results.asp?search=free+resources

PlanWare: www.planware.org/strategicplan.htm

Senge, P.M. (2006). *The fifth discipline: The art and practice of the learning organization*. New York: Doubleday.

Sloan, J. (2006). *Learning to think strategically*. Oxford, U.K.: Elsevier Science and Technology.

Chapter 13 *References*

Black, R.A. (2006). *Broken crayons: Break your crayons and draw Outside the lines*. Athens, GA: Self Published. Retrieved 26 August 2008 on http://www.cre8ng.com/brokencrayons.shtml

Klemm, W.R. (2001). *Leadership: Creativity and innovation*. p. 426-439. Concepts for Air Force Leadership (Second Ed.). Maxwell AFB, ALA: Air University.

Kouses, J.M. & Posner, B.Z. (2007). *The leadership challenge*. San Francisco, CA: Jossey-Bass.

Porter O'Grady, T. & Malloch, K. (2002). *Quantum Leadership*. Gaithersburg, MD: Aspen Publications.

Additional Leadership Development Resources

Business Network: http://resources.bnet.com/topic/creativity+and+innovation.html

Creativity and Innovation in the Workplace: www.business.com/directory/human_resources/workforce_management/creativity_and_innovation

Creativity Portal: www.creativity-portal.com

Creativity Web: http://www.members.optusnet.com.au/charles57/Creative/index2.html

Innovation resources: www.innovationtools.com

Van der Duin, P.A. (2004). Innovating for the future in *Thinking creatively in turbulent times.* Didsbury, H.F. (ed.) Bethesda, MD: World Futures Society.

Chapter 14 *References*

Armour, M. (2007). *Humility and leadership: No laughing matter*. Retrieved 26 August 2008 from http://qbsblog.wordpress.com/2007/08/25/dr-mike-armour-humility-and-leadership

Collins, J. (2001). *Good to great*. New York: HarperCollins Publishers.

Collins, J. & Porras, J. I. (2004). *Built to last*. New York: HarperCollins Publishers.

Additional Leadership Development Resources

Autry, J.A. (2004). *The servant leader*. New York" Three Rivers Press.

Greenleaf Center for Servant Leadership. Retrieved June 29, 2008 from www.greenleaf.org

Humility: http://www.mindtools.com/pages/article/newLDR_69.htm

Palmer. P. (2000). *Let your life speak*. San Francisco, CA: Jossey-Bass.

Pelletier, J. (2008). *Applying humility and strong professional willpower to leadership*. Retrieved 26 August 2008 from www.12manage.com/methods_collins_level_5_leadership.html

Servant Leadership: www.servantleadership.org

Chapter 15 *References*

Heathfield, S.M. (2008). *Ten pathways to show appreciation to employees and co-workers*. Retrieved June 29, 2008 from http://humanresources.about.com/cs/rewardrecognition/a/appreciation.htm

Kouzes, J.M. & Posner, B.Z. (2007). *The leadership challenge*. San Francisco, CA: Jossey-Bass.

Nelson, B., Blanchard, K. & Schudlich, S. (1994). *1001 ways to reward employees*. New York: William Morrow Co.

Porter-O'Grady, T. & Malloch, K. (2002). *Quantum leadership*. Gaithersburg, MD: Aspen Publications.

Additional Leadership Development Resources

Guiding Principles of Employee Recognition: http://www.washington.edu/admin/hr/roles/mgr/ee-recognition/guiding-principles.html

Human Resources Management: www.managementhelp.org

Kurth, K. & Schmidt, s. (2003). *Running on plenty at work*. VA: Renewal Resources Press.

Recognition Concepts: http://www.recognitionconcepts.com/

Recognition Ideas: www.baudville.com/articles.asp?v=all&c=6

Recognition Professionals International. Retrieved June 29, 2008 from www.recognition.org

Society for Human Resource Management. Retrieved June 25, 2008 from www.shrm.org

Index

CALLING ALL NURSE LEADERS

The Honor Society of Nursing, Sigma Theta Tau International has the resources you need to take your leadership skills to the next level!

LEADERSHIP BOOKS:

These books are helping nurses make pivotal changes in the nursing profession – one leader at a time.

Conversations With Leaders: Frank Talk From Nurses (and Others) on the Front Lines of Leadership

A Daybook for Nurse Leaders and Mentors

Pivotal Moments in Nursing: Leaders Who Changed the Path of a Profession, Vol. I & II

To find out more information about these and other honor society publications visit www.nursingknowledge.org/stti/books

NURSE MANAGER CERTIFICATE PROGRAM:

The Nurse Manager Certificate Program is a Web-based educational tool that helps nurses develop management competencies needed to be successful in today's fast-paced, ever-changing health care environment. These courses use the latest evidence-based information and will help nurses build successful teams, think strategically and become better project managers.

Topics include Budgeting, Patient and Worker Safety, Team Building, Project Management and more!

Ideal for schools of nursing, health care organizations and individuals.

For more information, contact Nursing Knowledge International at 1.888.NKI.4YOU or via e-mail at solutions@nursingknowledge.org

LEADERSHIP PROGRAMS:

Discover. Grow. Lead.

Achieve your leadership potential and pursue your professional goals.

The International Leadership Institute offers leadership programs, mentoring opportunities and career development resources designed to improve leadership skills and develop nurses' unique gifts and talents, including:

Board Leadership Development
Mentored Leadership Development
Maternal-Child Health Leadership Academy
Geriatric Nursing Leadership Academy
CareerMap

To learn more about the leadership programs visit www.nursingsociety.org/LeadershipInstitute

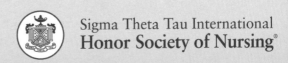

Sigma Theta Tau International
Honor Society of Nursing

Call for Global Online Course Authors

The Honor Society of Nursing, Sigma Theta Tau International invites nurses worldwide to participate as course authors for the honor society's online education programs.

Give back to the nursing community and become an online course author!

Course authors provide the content for online continuing education courses — then honor society staff transforms that content into an interactive learning tool.

Nurses use these online courses:
- As a teaching tool
- To support their work in clinical settings
- To enhance their professional lives
- To renew their career

Nursing topic areas include but are not limited to:
- Career Development (at all career stages)
- Complementary Health
- Cultural Diversity
- Disaster and Bioterrorism
- Environmental Health
- Evidence-Based Practice
- Ethics
- Geriatrics
- Global Nursing
- Informatics
- Health Care Policy
- Leadership and Mentoring
- Patient Safety
- Public Health
- Research and Scholarship
- Technology

While these are the key areas of focus, the honor society welcomes course material with content and in languages specific to regional and global needs.

For more information about participating in course development and to receive an application packet, please e-mail education@stti.iupui.edu or visit www.nursingsociety.org.

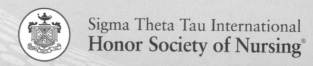

Sigma Theta Tau International
Honor Society of Nursing®